No Fear for My People

By Jill Shannon

MANIFEST
PUBLICATIONS

No Fear for My People

Copyright © 2019 Jill Shannon

ALL RIGHTS RESERVED WORLDWIDE

Manifest International, LLC
www.manifestinternational.com

ISBN: 978-1-951280-00-0

Unless otherwise indicated, all Scripture is taken from the New King James Version®. Copyright © 1982 by Thomas Nelson, Inc. Used by permission. All rights reserved.

Scriptures noted "NIV" are taken from the HOLY BIBLE, NEW INTERNATIONAL VERSION® Copyright © 1973, 1978, 1984 by International Bible Society. Used by permission of Zondervan. All rights reserved.

Scriptures noted "KJV" are taken from the King James Version, public domain.

Scriptures noted "AP" are the author's own translation or paraphrase.

Scriptures in bold print are the author's emphasis.

Cover Art Painting: "Presence" by Nancy DeWind
Graphic Design by Dave Gerhart

Other Books by Jill Shannon

Coffee Talks with Messiah: When Intimacy Meets Revelation
Evergreen Press, 2007

A Prophetic Calendar: The Feasts of Israel
Destiny Image Publishers, 2009

The Seduction of Christianity: Overcoming the Lukewarm Spirit of the Church
Destiny Image Publishers, 2010

Israel's Prophetic Destiny: If I Forget Jerusalem
Destiny Image Publishers, 2012

Unveiling the Song of Songs
Xulon Press, 2014

The Priestly Songwriter: Partnering with the Lord to Write Songs from Heaven
Xulon Press, 2017

Endorsements

Over the years, I have read and studied on the subject of fear in scripture. The fear of man becomes a snare, keeping one from fulfilling and attaining to their greatest potential in this life. The lack of the fear of the LORD in the context of scripture becomes an even greater snare in an age of never-ending temptation and apostasy.

My friend Jill Shannon, through her transparent and open examination of her own life and her exegesis of scripture, has unlocked a treasure in the revelation she brings. It is as timely as it is needed in this hour. Of all the works I've read to date, this is by far the most graspable and revelatory examinations on this subject I've ever seen.

To all who are students of life as well as the Word, this is a must-read. If taken to heart it will set you free to become an instrument of great holiness and power in this hour. Thank you, Jill, for your obedience in writing this. May the Lord continue to speak through you in such depth in the future!

Dr. Bruce D. Allen
Still Waters International Missions

Once again, our dearly beloved sister, Jill Shannon, has written a book which is a rich and wide-ranging study of Fear, and how to effectually overcome its stranglehold over us.

Through Scriptures and many real testimonies, Jill illustrates to us that even the feeblest vessels have all the power and authority they need, given freely by our dear Lord Jesus, to stand triumphant, even in the gloomiest of circumstances. This precious, divinely-inspired book will surely encourage you. You will not feel lonesome and stranded in your fears anymore; rather, you will know we are all standing together in this fight.

Sadhu Sundar Selvaraj
CMD, Jesus Ministries
Angel Broadcasting Network

Jill Shannon knows firsthand what it is like to be tormented by a spirit of fear. She also knows what it is like to see fear crushed under her feet and to walk in the supernatural peace of God. Yes, it is the "God of peace" who will "crush satan's head underneath your feet" (Romans 16:20), and Jill can show you how. She will lead you, step by step, into victory over fear.

Pastor Joseph Sweet
Shekinah Worship Center
Lancaster, CA

This book is a veritable banquet in God's Word! Jill imparts very powerful revelation for our time, regarding that one problem from which we all seem to suffer: FEAR! I have come to realize that fear is the favorite tool in the enemy's toolbox, which he uses to distract us, to paralyze us, and ultimately to destroy our faith.

In this book, Jill addresses so many important, timely issues that we all face as we transition from this age to the Kingdom age. Through Scripture, she helps us to understand the importance of knowing and stepping into our fore-ordained assignments on this earth, boldly and courageously fulfilling our destinies. To successfully do this, we must overcome our fears, and Jill has given us a literal Scriptural road map to help us find the way.

In sharing the powerful stories and testimonies of her own experiences with the demonic realm, Jill offers the reader very up-close and personal examples of how the enemy tempts us into horrific fears in order to compel us to abandon our faith in Yeshua the Messiah. As His return draws nearer and nearer, the enemy knows his days are short and the battle for the souls of believers is intensified. This book truly is filled with the "armor" every child of God needs to overcome to the end!

One paragraph cut deep to my heart and revealed to me what the Holy Spirit wants to do in me personally to overcome my own deep-seated fear. The Word of the Lord in 1 John 4:17 immersed my soul in a holy conviction and a wondrous revelation! *"Love has been perfected among us in this: that we may have boldness in the day of judgment; because as He is, so are we in this world."* Jill wrote, "John is telling us that when love is perfected in us, we can face the Day of Judgment without fear or regret. We can boldly stand before the Lord because His love will have been made perfect in us, if we allow Him." This one powerful truth shattered the chains that have held my heart in bondage to fear! The Scriptures regarding the Final Judgment Seat of Messiah have always been terribly fearful to me. And even though I realize that some of that is a healthy fear (awe) of our God, there was also a lack of perfection in the love of my heart toward people in my life. I was very deeply convicted to resolve this, in order to allow the Lord (as Jill says) to do this great, final work of cleansing in me, as I prepare to become the pure, spotless Bride that Yeshua is coming to redeem. This truth alone gave me Spirit-filled power to overcome fear as I am perfected in Love.

I know there will be striking, life-changing revelations for each one who holds and reads this book. May the Spirit of God speak to you, as He did to me, to search out and find those fears that have kept you from all that God has planned for you!

Kelly Ferrari Mills
Doorkeeper Ministries
www.doorkeeperministries.com

"No Fear for My People" is a highly valuable book, with powerful tools for anyone who desires to mature in the Lord. You will grow spiritually, be set free, and overcome the spirit of fear. I could not put this book down! Jill Shannon hits the target in the center – she delves into the hidden battleground of the human soul – FEAR!

True to her well-known transparency and in-depth style, Jill digs deeper into the biblical understandings and contexts of fear, and she opens up her heart and her own life experiences to us, like a rare and trusted friend that only God would send us. Jill exposes the fears that could sabotage our destiny in God, and then gives us the strategies to face them head-on, with trust and intimacy with our one and only Yeshua.

This book will leave you clothed in strength, armed with the Word of God, and adorned with holiness. We will need these spiritual weapons, as we approach the days of darkness to come. I advise you to absorb this book as a banquet of wisdom, faith, and truth: "Eat, O friends! Drink, yes, drink deeply, O beloved ones!" (SOS 5:1).

Catherine Minnick
Sr. Chaplain, IFOC

In this "treasure manual" for overcoming and conquering fear, Jill has brilliantly unlocked hidden Biblical truths for every believer in these last days.

But instead of testifying to the 'must-read' quality of this book, needed by everyone who has struggled with fear on any level, I'd like to testify to the author herself.

Jill Shannon is one of the most transparent, sincere, devoted, and obedient (to the Lord) teachers that walks the earth. I have known her for over two decades and have had the privilege of having her as a dear friend and mentor for over ten years. She is the real deal, who not only talks the talk but walks the walk. The anointing that the Holy Spirit pours out upon her as she teaches, whether in person or on paper, is manifested in each and every word. She lives under the fear of the Lord and desires to please Him alone, with all of her heart.

I don't believe you will find an easier or more effective book on battling fear, because this is straight from the heart of Lord Yeshua. He shares His heart through Jill, so we can ALL overcome fear today and in the days ahead.

Tanya Newman
Teacher, Intercessor

Contents

Chapter 1:	A Biblical Overview of Fear............	1
Chapter 2:	A Life of Fear	14
Chapter 3:	The Many Meanings of Fear	28
Chapter 4:	Do Not Fear Them – I AM With You!	37
Chapter 5:	Worry and Anxiety	49
Chapter 6:	Who is On the Lord's Side?	55
Chapter 7:	Discovering Our Destiny................	72
Chapter 8:	The Fear of the Lord	86
Chapter 9:	The Judgment Seat of Messiah	103
Chapter 10:	Warfare in the Spirit Realm	116
Epilogue:	....	136
Meditation on Scripture:	....	138
Appendix:	The Millennium.........................	142

Chapter 1
A Biblical Overview of Fear

My soul, wait silently for God alone,
For my expectation is from Him.
He alone is my rock and my salvation;
He is my defense; and I shall not be moved.
Psalm 62:5

My Heart for This Book

I would never have chosen to write a book about overcoming fear. I consider myself to be one of the most anxious and fearful people I know. However, the Lord has begun to teach me the spiritual principles of overcoming fear. I'm learning how to fight this battle and I've seen it is possible to win. But it's not easy, and I'm not there yet.

I believe the emotion of fear – the involuntary chemistry of fear – the relentless grip of the spirit of fear – is one of the greatest enemies of our souls in the course of our lives. It can cripple us, and prevent us from taking necessary action. Fear is torment.

*There is no fear in love; but perfect love casts out fear, because **fear involves torment**. But he who fears has not been made perfect in love* (1Jn.4:18).

Fear challenges us in our journey as believers, as overcomers, as parents, and as the Lord's priestly army on the earth. Being continually afraid while serving as a soldier in an army, whether an earthly or heavenly army, seems incompatible. And yet the Bible often tells us that we are soldiers, fighting an epic spiritual battle against the powers of darkness, and against all that hinders the message of Salvation from reaching the nations and His people Israel.

The Lord directed me to write this book. First, in the middle of the night, I heard a heavenly voice singing audibly into my ear, an urgent invitation for the Lord to be **near to us**. Then a few minutes later, after writing down the music and words I had heard, I saw in my mind the title of a book: "No Fear for My People." Then I saw someone writing a review of this book, which did not yet exist. I delayed beginning to write, due to my lack of qualification in overcoming fear. I have continual battles with fear, and often, fear wins!

But in obedience, I write, and by God's grace, He will help me to overcome fear, even as I am writing this to help others overcome fear.

A Kingdom Principle

Sometimes God chooses the unqualified, and if they obey, in the very process of obeying the Lord, they become qualified. Gideon is a good example. The Lord called him a "mighty man of valor" when he was hiding in the winepress, threshing wheat out of sight of the marauding Midianites. Gideon felt like a weak coward, but when he obeyed the Lord, he became the most qualified leader in Israel to destroy the Midianites. Actually, the Lord did all the heavy lifting. But Gideon had to overcome fear first and go out to meet the enemy, and God qualified him. May it also be for all of us who overcome our fear and win the battle, by the Lord's strong deliverance. Amen.

Each time we fight and gain a victory over one particular aspect of fear, e.g., fear of rejection, fear of cancer, fear of death or martyrdom, fear of plane crashes, fear of poverty in old age – we gain Divine authority to help others fighting similar challenges. It only takes "just one man," or "just one woman" to overcome all odds and win; immediately, others will follow and do similar exploits.

For example, respected teacher and prophet Neville Johnson has shared that once we have overcome a certain disease or affliction, we now have authority over that disease as we pray for others to overcome the same thing. I've seen this work in my own life; when I finally achieve breakthrough in a certain area of healing, fear, intimacy or faith, I can then impart it to others, through my love for them and my simple prayers. As I write this book for you, I am not only instructing but also imparting to you that which I have begun to overcome. But I am still on the journey.

We even see this principle in the Olympic games. The moment one runner breaks the record for the first time in history, others begin to rise up to match this record-breaking time, and then to exceed it. When a certain ice-skater performed the world's first "Triple Axel," (named after Norwegian skater Axel Paulsen, who performed this jump in 1882), it then encouraged all other skaters to come up to this new standard of qualification.

Another example is seen when King Saul's armies were challenged by the barbaric Philistine forces. The Israelite soldiers were paralyzed with fear. The Philistine champion towered over normal men, and he was loaded with enormous weapons, as befitting his stature. None of Saul's men had the confidence or courage to face the giant. Certain death awaited any soldier foolish enough to confront this man who was almost twice their height and weight, as were his weapons. For 40 days, Goliath taunted and humiliated Saul and his men.

And then young David came to the troops, bearing gifts of food for the trapped army. When David asked about the situation, they mocked and scorned this young and inexperienced lad for daring to suggest that someone could beat the dread Philistine strongman.

However, David displayed an almost impossible lack of fear for his personal safety. He knew that Israel's God would support him in his bold but unlikely attempt to defeat him. We all know the story. The moment David singlehandedly stoned the hulking and arrogant warrior and quickly cut off his massive head, the entire Israelite army suddenly became the bravest and most confident of soldiers. And the brave Philistine army suddenly became a band of sniveling cowards and ran for their sorry lives.

Once David overcame fear, he gave the army this overcoming spirit. David overcame fear through his confidence in God, and this overcoming spirit was contagious. David's victory imparted this same courage to the whole army.

Once we overcome fear in a certain area, we now have authority from the Lord to help others battling the same fears.

Does the Lord Understand our Fears?

There are so many things to be afraid of. I guess we could spend a whole chapter just listing and describing the many things we fear, both rational and irrational; from car accidents to cancer, from spiders to nuclear war, from humiliation to getting fired from our job, and the list goes on. We probably won't waste the time making this long list, but will use our time in a more healing and productive way.

Let's think about the Lord's perspective. He continually admonishes us to be courageous and not to fear, and yet, **He understands there is much to be afraid of.** The Lord deeply understands our fears, and He is compassionate towards us. But His loving heart will continually counsel and encourage us to move forward, despite the fear. *He doesn't require the absence of fear – rather, He requires that we walk forward into His* *assignments out of obedience and trust, whether the fear still grips us or not.*

He saw His original human creations – His masterpieces of workmanship – Adam and Eve, just after they had tragically tasted the fruit of the Tree of the Knowledge of Good and Evil. Their immediate response was to be **afraid** of Him who had made them in love. And they hid themselves out of His sight, covered in fig leaves and trembling in fear to face Him. Moments before, they had been unafraid, unashamed, and innocent. Intimate with their Maker and running freely through the garden in the sunlight, and resting under the shade of lofty trees.

Beloved, **all** the fears we have ever faced and will ever face, are the direct result of eating of the knowledge of Good and Evil. Not only did Adam and Eve eat of it, but all of us have eaten of it, in one way or another. And each of us has been subjected, unwillingly, to its consequences (see Rom.8:19-21). One of the cruelest consequences of knowing Good and Evil is FEAR. Death was the consequence of the knowledge of Good and Evil and the fear of death is the root of all fears. The Lord Yeshua came to set us free from the bondage of the fear of death (see Heb. 2:15).

It's true that innocent babies have not known good and evil in any conscious way, and we would think they should be exempt from this curse, but the Bible tells us that we were conceived in sin and born into sin. So even innocent children are somehow subjected to this syndrome, and all too soon, they learn fear.

Modern technology has shown us the most shocking videos and ultrasound images of an unborn baby still growing in the womb, displaying fear, just before the instruments of abortion are introduced to its mother's womb. The fear is evident in its facial expressions, its shrinking back from the instrument, and the elevated heartbeat of its fear.

I saw a six-minute film depicting this reality, called "Hard Truth." When I watched it, my soul went into severe shock at the horror, which was now impossible to deny. I felt like I was in hell when I watched this film, beholding what our society has become, and what human carnage it has allowed. I hope I never recover so that my conscience will never grow hard and cold again. Seeing this reality in medical video footage leaves the permanent scars of outrage, grief, and horror in any soul who watches it. One can also view ultrasound imagery and learn more medical facts about the unborn, in a recently released movie (as of the writing of this book), "Unplanned." My main point here is that even the innocent unborn can still experience fear, which is both remarkable and sad.

But the purpose of this book is not to glorify fear or sink into depression. This message is a word of HOPE, HEALING, FREEDOM, and REDEMPTION from the torment of FEAR.

It is redemptive, and the Lord has commissioned this book so that many of His people will be set free from fear, even if we live through the darkest night of human history. It will also be the brightest light of human history, shining out from those who have overcome, by the word of our testimony, by the power of His blood, and by not valuing the preserving of our own lives more than standing firm on the Word of Truth.

The Courage of the Lord

The Lord Yeshua is the most courageous and heroic Person in the Universe, unashamedly and unswervingly correcting, confronting, rebuking, and defeating His enemies. The leaders and members of His own hometown synagogue were enraged at His blunt rebuke of their unbelieving spirit, comparing them to their ancestors in the generations of Elijah and Elisha (see Lk.4:17-30).

In their offense, they dragged Him out to the cliff at the edge of town, to dash Him against the rocks below. The Lord knew this was not His destiny moment to give His life and somehow, He walked right through the murderous mob, against all odds, and went His way. I don't know how He accomplished this miracle, but it required faith – and fear and faith cannot operate together.

The Lord Yeshua, during His days on earth, lived out this exemplary level of courage in many aspects of His life, and also in His torturous and humiliating interrogations and death, when the appointed time had come.

He displayed courage when He boldly and not-too-diplomatically confronted the most respected ruling religious powers of His day. Because Yeshua was willingly submitted to His Father, He said only what His Father was saying, and Yeshua knew how these words would offend and insult the listeners, who were the most pious and biblically-educated men in their generation. These were the spiritual leaders of Israel in His day! Do you think it was easy for Him to pronounce these harsh rebukes, even when He was having a nice meal at a Pharisee's house, with many friends and leaders gathered? Couldn't He just enjoy the meal and be nice?

Did you ever read some of His words, and privately think, "Lord, why did You have to say that so harshly? You could have made it softer or kinder." In our polite society, His blunt rebukes might appear to us as rude. Honestly, I've had those thoughts, reading the gospels. Maybe you have too. But I now realize that the Lord was saying exactly what the Father was burdening Him to say, and Yeshua could feel His Father's emotions as He spoke those words.

In the Old Testament, His Father said some equally harsh and insulting things. Isn't this why they stoned the prophets of old, and why the king had Isaiah sawn in half? The Son, as the exact representation of His Father, did what His Father showed Him, during His days on earth. And if the rebuke stung, it was meant to accomplish repentance in the listener, though in many cases, they responded in prideful anger.

The Lord was courageous, but do not think He didn't have to overcome fear. I'm certain He did. He had to overcome *everything* we struggle with (see Heb. 4:15). Do not suppose that His courage was merely the absence of fear. No, it was feeling the fear, but obeying what the Father required, regardless of possible consequences. This is true courage. This is actually the Fear of the Lord.

*For in that He Himself has suffered, being tempted, He is able to aid those who are tempted...For we do not have a High Priest who cannot sympathize with our weaknesses, but was in **all points** tempted as we are, yet without sin* (Heb.2:18, 4:15).

The common people loved Yeshua, but many were too **afraid** that the Pharisees would evict them from the synagogue and from the larger Jewish community; that they would be cut off from their livelihood, surrounded by the cruel and powerful Roman military government (see Jn.12:42). They greatly **feared** being excommunicated from the synagogue and all the social networking and protection that this system afforded Jewish families in that Roman-occupied territory.

But not Yeshua. He knew He would be rejected but did not shrink back from speaking the whole truth. He stood before His tormentors and those who insulted Him, speaking truth to the end, loving them to the end. He was and is the bravest Man we will ever know. My heart melts at His bravery in the face of such scorn, insult, shame, and cruelty.

*Therefore Jesus also, that He might sanctify the people with His own blood, suffered outside the gate. Therefore let us go forth to Him, **outside the camp, bearing His reproach**. For here we have no continuing city, but we seek the one to come* (Heb.13:12-14).

Can the Lord Ever Be Afraid?

Could the Lord God ever be afraid of anything? And if so, what could He possibly be afraid of, since He has all power and all knowledge? We would automatically answer, "No, the Lord is not afraid of anything."

However, in one sense, He and all of heaven are also afraid of something. Afraid of a day that is coming. Afraid of a night that is far spent. Afraid of having to pronounce and execute punishments that will cause His heart inexpressible agony. Afraid of what will happen to those who think they know Him, but in truth, they do not and are deceiving themselves. I believe His loving heart dreads the pain of "That Day."

Because of God's great love for all people, He feels what we feel, even our regrets and shame; He shares our pain, and our tears become His tears. He suffers when unbelievers are sent to eternal punishment, or when casual, "lukewarm believers" suffer loss and unbearable regret at the Judgment Seat of Messiah. (We will study the Judgment Seat of Messiah in Chapter 9.)

The Prophets warn us often of the day of judgment, and they are not always writing to unbelievers, but rather to God's people, who believe they are in right standing with Him. This is one example from Amos.

"Woe to you who desire the day of the LORD! For what good is the day of the LORD to you? It will be darkness, and not light. It will be as though a man fled from a lion, and a bear met him! Or as though he went into the house, leaned his hand on the wall, and a serpent bit him! (Amos 5:18-19).

And in the New Testament, John warns us how strict are the Lord's standards for His people to qualify (see Rev.3:15-16). And Peter tells us it will be a fearful day, even for the righteous.

"If it is hard for the righteous to be saved, what will become of the ungodly and the sinner?" (1Pet.4:18, NIV).

Likewise, Ezekiel also warns us about how exacting and unrelenting will be His judgments.

Son of man, when a land sins against Me by persistent unfaithfulness, I will stretch out My hand against it; I will cut off its supply of bread, send famine on it, and cut off man and beast from it. **Even if these three men, Noah, Daniel, and Job, were in it, they would deliver only themselves by their righteousness,"** says the Lord God (Eze.14:13-14).

I think we can prove that God and His Heavenly Hosts can feel a type of fear, though it is not the same as our normal, human fear. But how could God be afraid? Let's look at some passages to explain this unexpected emotion in the heart of the Lord.

First, the Father expresses a unique type of **fear for His own Name and reputation**, in the following passage, predicting His fierce judgments upon disobedient Israel. This is one of the few places in the Bible where the Father expresses His fear for the consequences of His judgments:

*The sword shall destroy outside; there shall be terror within for the young man and virgin, the nursing child with the man of gray hairs. **I would have said, "I will dash them in pieces, I will make the memory of them to cease from among men," had I not feared the wrath of the enemy, lest their adversaries should misunderstand,** lest they should say, "Our hand is high; and it is not the Lord who has done all this."* (Deut. 32:25-28).

In this passage above, the Lord says He would have completely wiped out Israel as a nation, **but He feared** that the evil nations would misunderstand and think they had destroyed Israel by their own power and that the Lord had no power to save them – afraid that the enemies would misinterpret Israel's destruction and boast about it. The Lord was not willing for the enemies of Israel to come to that proud and mistaken conclusion. Therefore, He spared them, as a Father would spare His son, though Israel had sinned greatly.

Secondly, **the prophet Moses feared for God's reputation**, among the nations. This kind of intercessory fear – the fear that people will think evil things about the Lord's goodness – this type of godly fear pleases the Lord. He knows we don't want unbelievers to come to wrongful conclusions about His goodness.

*And the LORD said to Moses, "I have seen this people, and indeed it is a stiff-necked people! Now therefore, **let Me alone, that My wrath may burn** hot against them and **I may consume them.** And I will make of you a great nation."*

*Then Moses pleaded with the LORD his God, and said: "LORD, why does Your wrath burn hot against Your people whom You have brought out of the land of Egypt with great power and with a mighty hand? **Why should the Egyptians speak, and say, 'He brought them out to harm them, to kill them in the mountains, and to consume them from the face of the earth'?** Turn from Your fierce wrath, and relent from this harm to Your people* (Ex.32:9-12).

All Creation Groans

Thirdly, all of Heaven is afraid and shaken by the wickedness of Israel, and the consequential judgments that will come. Notice in this next passage that the Lord is not telling sinners to be afraid, but rather, He is speaking to His domain and His creation:

*"Be astonished, O heavens, at this, and **be horribly afraid**, be very desolate, says the Lord"* (Jer.2:12).

The Hebrew word for "horribly afraid" is *"s'ar,"* and Strong's Concordance gives us this definition: "To storm, shiver, dread, bristle (with horror), be very afraid."

The word "heavens" is *"shamayim,"* and can apply to the physical atmosphere far above the earth, as well as to the domain of God, the highest heaven.

The context of this passage is the apostasy of Israel. The Lord and His heavenly hosts are shocked, appalled, and afraid as they behold the wickedness of God's people. The very heavens tremble and are shaken when God's judgments come. The physical bodies in heaven are shaken and fall to the earth (see Mt.24:29, Rev.6:12-14).

The Lord cries out that His nation has changed their gods, who are not gods at all (see verse 11). And they have forsaken the spring of living water and dug their own cisterns, broken cisterns that cannot hold water (see verse 13).

What is Heaven afraid of? I believe Heaven is afraid of the necessary consequences for profound unfaithfulness, which the Lord is required to judge severely. He cannot bear to execute these punishments.

*"How can I give you up, Ephraim? How can I hand you over, Israel?...**My heart churns within Me;** My sympathy is stirred. I will not execute the fierceness of My anger"* (Hos.11:8-9a).

A parent can warn a child for years, but when the child gets big enough to make his own decision, the parent fears for the choices that child will make. The parent knows how terrible will be the consequences, but the child has free will when they come of age. And the child's disregard for the safety of the parent's instruction is going to bring destruction. And the parent watches with horror and fear.

Many dear parents reading this can understand the truth in it. We fear what the consequences of our children's disobedience or rebellion will bring. But the child has free will, and as they grow older and into adulthood, they can exercise this free will all the more.

Free will is the gift of God, and as long as we live on this earth, that free will continues. But at the time of death, or the Coming of the Lord, if a soul is not saved, its free will is taken away. At that point, the human soul has no further ability to choose its actions or its standing before God. Only the Lord, the Judge, can now determine its eternal position. But all the choices we make on this earth will directly affect the Lord's evaluation of our lives, and how we will be placed for all eternity.

All creation suffers and groans under the weight of our sin. And Heaven feels the pain of this. The Lord also weeps when innocent children are abused, starved, or murdered on the earth. He knows that ultimately, justice will be done; but not until the appointed time.

The Lord speaks in Isaiah 24 of the people's rebellion and disobedience. The earth is under a curse, and He unfolds terrible judgments on the earth to all people, and in the skies above. His heart does not desire these punishments, and He would plead that we not continue in our rebellion.

*Because they have transgressed the laws, changed the ordinance, **broken the everlasting covenant**. Therefore **the curse has devoured the earth**, and those who dwell in it are desolate…**The earth shall reel** to and fro like a drunkard, and shall totter like a hut; **its transgression shall be heavy upon it**, and it will fall, and not rise again* (Isa.24:5-6, 20).

The Fear of a Spiritual Father for His Children

In the same manner, the apostle Paul speaks of the consequences of man's sin and rebellion, affecting all creation. He knows that creation longs to be restored, and it will be the Lord's mature sons and daughters who will free it from the curse. In this passage from Romans, Paul seems to be commenting on Isaiah 24, but he offers new hope to the obedient children of God.

*For the earnest expectation of the **creation eagerly waits for the revealing of the sons of God**. For the creation was subjected to futility, not willingly, but because of Him who subjected it in hope; because the **creation itself also will be delivered** from the bondage of corruption into the **glorious liberty of the children of God**. For we know that **the whole***

creation groans and labors with birth pangs together until now (Rom.8:19-22).

Paul also expresses his **fear of the consequences** that will come to the churches he had established, as they had drifted away into carnality, false doctrines, and sin.

*I am **afraid for you**, lest I have labored for you in vain* (Gal.4:11).

And again, he expresses his **fatherly fear** toward the Corinthians' weaknesses.

*For **I am afraid** that when I come I may not find you as I want you to be, and you may not find me as you want me to be. **I fear** that there may be discord, jealousy, fits of rage, selfish ambition, slander, gossip, arrogance and disorder. **I am afraid** that when I come again my God will humble me before you, and **I will be grieved** over many who have sinned earlier and have not repented of the impurity, sexual sin and debauchery in which they have indulged.* (2 Cor.12:20-21).

Paul also expresses his **husbandly** jealousy and fear, as if he can feel God's jealous love for His bride, as a Husband who is afraid of their vulnerability to being seduced.

*For I am jealous for you with God's jealousy. For I have betrothed you to **one Husband**, that I may present you as a pure virgin to Christ. But **I fear** that somehow, **as the serpent deceived Eve by his craftiness, so your minds may be corrupted** from your single-minded devotion that is in Christ* (2Cor.11:2-3, AP).

The Lord Exhorts Us Not to Fear

We see in hundreds of Scriptures that the Lord does not want His people to be afraid. He has stated this continually in both the Old and New Covenants. Some scholars have calculated that the Lord has said, "Do not be afraid," no less than 365 times in the Bible, which covers every day of the year.

Clearly, we all have a strong need to be constantly encouraged, as we all have many reasons to be afraid. The Lord knows and understands our fears, which are the result of knowing good and evil, as we mentioned earlier. He does not want us to live in fear, but this is a hard enemy to overcome. May this book be one more tool, used by the Lord, to bring us to a new level of victory over fear, despite living amidst much turmoil and dangerous situations.

King David's Battles with Fear

King David shared his fears openly in many of his Psalms, and he thanked the Lord each time He was delivered him from the terrible dangers he faced and feared. His life was often in immediate peril, more peril than most of us will ever know. The same God who delivered him from Goliath, delivered him over and over, during years of running for his life and fighting countless wars. But when he had stood up against Goliath, as a young and unarmed shepherd lad, against all odds, **David had absolutely no fear at all!**

You might ask, "Why was David afraid during all those latter years when he could have remembered how God had delivered him from Goliath?"

This is a fair question. I believe the Spirit of the Lord overshadowed young David with supernatural confidence and courage to stand against the giant, with only a sling and a bag of stones (but one was enough!), wearing no armor whatsoever.

The Lord needed to raise up a deliverer for Israel to survive this present survival-level Philistine threat. He needed to prop up Saul in his instability and character weaknesses; He needed to grant deliverance for Israel's demoralized army from total defeat and long-term subjugation to the merciless and godless Philistines. He needed to demonstrate that the Lord alone is mighty to save, and He can use **one unarmed youth** to do the impossible because he put his trust in the Lord. This was a lesson about trust and about how much the Lord loved Israel.

David was a man after God's own heart, but this did not prevent him from living a life filled with mortal dangers, day and night. He had many battles, struggles, threats, and severe hardships to overcome, without succumbing to bitterness or turning away from his God. These tests and trials lasted at least seven years, and by some reckonings, it could have been nearly 15 years before he was actually made king.

Our Journey into Understanding

We also see two seemingly different, even opposite definitions of the word "fear" as used in the Bible. The Lord requires us to have "the Fear of the Lord," and this teaching will be covered in Chapter 8. We know that our Lord Yeshua had the Fear of the Lord. It was His delight, and this caused Him to be heard and honored by His Father (see Isa.11:2-3, Heb. 5:7). We'll look at this in more detail later.

In other cases, Scripture shows us that God expects his enemies, and even His own backsliding people, to fear Him (see Job 19:29, Isa.13:8, 19:17, 31:9, Jer.2:12, 42:16, Rom.13:4).

Some weeks ago, (as of this writing,) when the Lord showed me the title of this new book, I saw the words, "No Fear for My People." Therefore, I know the primary focus of this book will be the Lord's deliverance for all of us, from the predatory, relentless fear that devours our emotions, robs our future, plunders our peace, and sidetracks our noble destinies. I can only suppose that He asked me to do this because I am one of the weakest and most fearful people He has ever met! So I can relate to you, and you can relate to me.

Like all of you, I know many people who are afraid of many things. Some of them are close friends, some are acquaintances, some are people I have only met in ministry assignments, and one such person is – myself. I have a strong desire to set others free from this disabling and at times demonic spirit of fear, and in doing so, I myself will somehow be set free in this process. We will walk through it together. AMEN.

Chapter 2
A Life of Fear

*For God has not given us a spirit of fear
But of power and of love, and of a sound mind.
2 Timothy 1:7*

To open my own heart and weaknesses to you, please let me share a little about my life's journey; first, as a Jewish child, and then later, as a believer in the Lord. We will see the continual presence of fear in my thoughts, dreams, emotions, and body, which began relatively early in my childhood.

Before I share these negative situations in my life that made me a fearful person, let me say this first:

Some of those reading this book have likely suffered far more trauma than my entire life combined, including events like attacks, disasters, accidents, molestation, rape, diseases in themselves or loved ones, starvation or poverty, even persecution, depending on the nation/culture you were raised in.

So as you read a few "highlights" (or should we say, "lowlights") of my life that left me fearful, please know that I had a relatively easy, safe and sheltered life, compared to most of the people in this cruel and broken world. It is not God's fault that this world is cruel and broken. He made all things beautiful.

It is the power of sin that we know fear; the power of knowing good and evil. It is the devil's continual sabotage, theft, and destruction of all that is righteous and true, and his vile attempts to steal all the purity, uprightness, honor and beauty out of our lives – lives God created with love, and He predestined them for eternal glory with Him.

Therefore, even with all the benefits and "goodness" I was raised in, I was still quite damaged, and needed the Spirit of God to rescue me from this "body of death," and, (I will add), "this mind of fear." Amen.

I Bless My Parents

I also need to add one more thought: In the testimonies you will read in this chapter, there are several circumstances and commentaries I share, which might make my parents sound uncaring or irresponsible. They *were* responsible and loving parents and tried to protect me in all the ways they knew how. I want you to know that I loved and honored my parents, though they did not know the Lord, and later, opposed my faith over many years.

My parents did the best they could when I was growing up, given their lack of understanding of biblical truth and absolute standards. Of course, they were "good people," from a humanistic worldview, and they acted according to what they knew and believed, some of which was unbiblical. I share these stories below not to dishonor them in any way, as that would be wrong. I honor and love my parents and cherish their memory. However, the Lord wants me to be transparent with you about why I grew up with such a tremendous undercurrent of fear in my thoughts, dreams, and decision-making.

My Early Journey

I was raised in a mostly secular Jewish background, with my father being more connected to his Judaism than my mother was to hers. I attended synagogue on holidays and was sent to Hebrew school for a few years, but this training only played a small role in forming my beliefs and attitudes.

My father, through his Jewish background, told me about the existence of God when I was about 5, and I am incredibly grateful for this. It gave me a foundation of knowing that God exists, even though he didn't talk about God in everyday conversations. Still, he had a certain spirituality, which was far better than atheism.

However, he got into a darker (false) spirituality, which he attempted to impose on me as a child and into my teen years. For some reason, I instinctively resisted my father's version of spirituality, even as a child; I can only think the Lord was protecting me, knowing I was going to be saved later. My mother did not seem to believe in God at all, but I grateful that at least my dad told me there was a God.

I later received the Lord after starting college away from home. More details about my salvation, life struggles, and intimacy with the Lord, can be found in my first book, "Coffee Talks with Messiah."

My parents loved and pampered me during my earliest years. They found me adorable, bright, inquisitive, and enthusiastic, and I'm sure those years were carefree. I was their delight, and I enjoyed the happiness and innocence of early childhood, which many readers can relate to. (Except for many precious readers, who were tragically born into abusive homes; in these cases, they never felt safe or carefree, from their earliest memories.) Please know that I have tremendous compassion for those who endured years of pain, shame, and constant fear, from having been abused from a young age. For those with this terrible history, some of my introductory remarks about my loving (although secular) childhood may seem insensitive, as if "feeling safe as a toddler is the norm."

Feeling safe as a young child *should* be the norm, of course. But for those who were physically, mentally, or sexually abused, it was anything but safe. For now, I will not be addressing the issues of childhood abuse, but will rather be speaking about the origins of fear in one who was not abused as a child. There were subtle forms of mental and even spiritual abuse in my home, but I will not be sharing them here.

There are many resources that address the specific needs of those who suffered cruel abuses in their youngest and formative years, and my heart is with you. May you receive all the help possible, from those competent counselors and authors who focus on victims of abuse. This book is more aimed at the general culture of fear instilled in many of us, who were not abused, or at least not in an obvious or outward way. However, I believe that readers who were abused as children and teens can very much benefit from this book, because so much of what I will share is common to all, whether we have a history of childhood abuse or not.

I don't remember exactly when I started to feel afraid, but here are a few of my first early memories:

1) When I was about 3-4 years old, I was playing with my younger toddler cousin in the snow, and I pushed him down deliberately. It was a mean thing to do, but I did it anyway. To this day, I don't know what I was thinking, or why I did that, since I loved him. Since he was bundled up in his thick snowsuit, and he only fell down about 4 inches, to sit in the snow, he certainly didn't get hurt. However, I didn't know that my dad was watching us play from an upstairs window. When he saw me doing this mean thing, he called out from the window that I would get a spanking when I came inside. I had never had a spanking before, and to the best of my memory, I might not have had another after this. But I was afraid to come inside from playing, afraid of the spanking. So I felt fear of my dad's punishment. That's my first memory.

2) About a year or two later, I was playing outside with my dad in the backyard. I fell into a little pit that was filled with ants, and the ants started swarming all over me. I was very afraid and pleaded for my dad to pull me out of the pit, but he started laughing, as if it looked so funny to see me in there, with the ants crawling on me. I don't know why that struck him as funny, but he laughed for what seemed to be a long time,

though it was probably about a minute. It was traumatic for me that he didn't immediately pull me out. I'm not sharing this to dishonor my dad, but that was my second memory of feeling fear. He pulled me out fairly soon, but not soon enough for me to feel safe.

3) My Jewish parents enrolled me in a private religious (not Jewish) school for kindergarten. I don't know why, but I guess they thought it was a better school than the public school. When I reached 1st grade, I had a mean teacher, and we were all afraid of her.

There was a boy in my class who had hemophilia, and he missed school a lot, due to this disease. One day, the teacher started yelling at the boy for missing school several days in a row. I thought she was being unfair, and I just blurted out, "But he can't help it if he's sick." In my family, if a child was sick, he or she had a right to stay home from school. At age 6, I was already defending this boy, without even asking permission to speak.

The teacher immediately punished me. She stood me up, yelled at me, taped my mouth with a piece of scotch tape, and put me in a dark closet in the back of the classroom. In that dark closet was a large, black spider in the upper corner. I had to stand there for an hour, staring at that spider, and terrified it would come after me. It stayed in the corner, but that was a very frightening experience.

When the teacher finally brought me out and pulled the tape off my mouth, I didn't want to let anyone know how scared I was, so I smiled bravely as if nothing traumatic had happened. When I got home from school, I told my mother what the teacher did to me, and I don't think she ever talked to the teacher about it. Looking back on it, what that teacher did was abusive, but back in those days, such a phrase as "abuse" was unheard of.

I realize that some readers may also have been placed in religious or church schools in their childhood, and sadly, some religious schools have been known for cruelty and abuse. This terrible reality is not the purpose of this book, but many readers know what I'm talking about.

Fear Breeds Hate, but Love Overcomes Fear

After my unpleasant experience in 1st grade, my elementary school years were mostly "safe." However, 3rd grade brought another challenge. My parents moved me to the public school to start 3rd grade, and my large class was given a new and inexperienced teacher who got violently angry often. She was a young, blonde, attractive teacher, but we were all afraid of her temper. She would line us up next to her desk, and then one by one, she would hurl our homework books out across the floor, as a sign of anger and disgust, without even looking at our homework to see if we had done it right. (O happy memories!)

Oddly, when 3rd grade was finally over, the teacher told my mother that she was fond of me and thought I was a model student. I had thought she hated all of us, but when school was over, she said nice things about me to my mother. Who knew?

As the summer vacation began, my mother wanted me to write a letter to her, thanking her for her year of teaching and congratulating her on becoming pregnant with her first baby (which meant she was not returning to school the following year.) Even though my parents were not remotely Christian in their beliefs or attitudes, I feel that something redemptive happened to me at age 8.

As secular Jews, we never talked about forgiveness or redemption. Privately, I hated my 3rd grade teacher all year, because I was afraid of her. Fear breeds hatred. The last thing I wanted to do was THANK HER for the year of 3rd grade, or to say something nice about her new baby on the way. I thought she would be the meanest mommy in the world to that new baby. But my mother urged me to write a nice note (I don't know why!) Even then, the Lord was working on me, as a child, though I wouldn't get saved for 11 more years.

Some type of grace and mercy came upon me, to write a loving "thank you" note to this teacher. I actually felt genuine love come into my heart as I wrote this sincere letter of thanks and wishing her the best with her new baby. Isn't that amazing? My mother mailed it, and this young teacher was deeply moved by what I wrote. With the school year now over, she became almost like a "friend" by mail, saying nothing but compliments to me in her letters.

Maybe the classroom of 30 kids was too much for her, but individually, maybe she was a really nice lady. I share this because I learned that fear brings hatred of the one you fear. **And love conquers both hatred and fear.** Having never heard the Bible, nor known the Lord, I learned this biblical truth through this life experience. I believe the Lord orchestrated this to teach me about forgiveness, and that "Perfect love casts out fear." AMAZING.

Fear of Plane Crashes

My parents sent me to day camp every summer, from an early age. Each child was assigned to a group of kids our own age, who all shared a little cabin called a "bunk." This was where we changed our clothes for swimming, played games, ate snacks, and had talks with our camp counselor. This event I'm sharing with you happened when I was nine years old.

One Monday morning, returning to camp after the weekend, the counselor came in and called us all to sit down together. She asked us if we had heard about "the plane accident." I thought she said, "the playing accident," meaning that some child had slipped and fallen while playing. That was the only kind of accident I could imagine.

She then told us that one of our own girls from our bunk had been killed in a "plane accident" the day before, which was a Sunday. I couldn't begin to understand what she was saying. I then noticed that this girl wasn't present in the bunk that day, but my mind couldn't grasp that she had been killed in some kind of accident – something I couldn't imagine or understand. That day was a blur of confusion and fear, and I was afraid to ask any questions.

My parents had never talked to me about death before. No one I knew had ever died at that point. Jewish families generally don't ever talk about death, until someone actually dies. And even then, they have no idea what to tell the children. I never learned about heaven or any spiritual aspect to human life, so this was just a blank spot in my mind.

When I got home, I can't remember if I asked my mother about it, but I picked up the newspaper my mother always had on the kitchen table. To my shock, I saw a photograph of that 10-year old girl from my bunk, with her name under the picture.

I was a good reader, and I carefully read the article over and over. This girl was at a swim club that Sunday. Since her parents were not listed among the dead, it was not clear to me if they were there too, or if their daughter had gone with another friend and her family.

This club had a large building for the members to change into their bathing suits, shower, or get dressed after swimming. A sudden storm came up, and many people ran to take shelter in the bathhouse. At that moment, a military plane burst into flames in the air above them, while attempting a landing at a nearby Naval base. (Looking back on it now, perhaps the plane was hit by lightning.) The pilot ejected out safely, but the plane crashed into that bathhouse.

As a child reading it, I didn't understand that it was a military plane, or how a plane just fell out of the sky, since the article didn't mention why it was burning. In the writing of this book now, I checked back online and researched this accident for the first time, and learned additional facts now, so many decades later.

The article explained that ten people died in this crash: seven adults and four children, including my friend. The article also showed a picture of the destroyed building, and possibly the wreckage of the plane as well.

There was no way I could understand this event, or what it meant that she was killed. My parents did not discuss it with me, nor did they help me process this. They didn't believe in the afterlife, so there was nothing they could say about death and remained silent on the matter.

Needless to say, for years I remained fearful of an airplane randomly falling out of the sky onto whatever building I was in. Later in life, when I had to fly for my jobs and other purposes, I was always afraid of the plane crashing. I didn't let the fear stop me from flying, but the fear was always there.

I know many people fear plane crashes, and it is very understandable, though thousands of flights a day are blessedly safe, and most people never experience a crash. But many of us grow up knowing that "our plane" might be the rare one that crashes.

Late in my life, after flying many dozens of times, and with help from the Lord, I have mostly overcome this gripping terror of my plane crashing. I have learned to entrust my life and protection to the Lord, who will decide the length of my life, based on His will for me and the assignments He has for me to accomplish.

I still fight the fear during times of turbulence, and recently, I instinctively grabbed the arm of the stranger next to me, when things got rough. I apologized to him about 30 seconds later, when I let go of his arm. And of course, I pray before every plane takes off!

The Cold War

There were a number of fear factors that began to grow in me, both privately at home, and culturally. By the time I was 10 or 11, I lived with a growing fear of evil – evil which took many forms in our culture. During the early 1960s, the U.S. entered a period of high enmity with the Soviet Union (now Russia.) Our two nations were in a nuclear arms race, and there was a real threat of a nuclear war between us. They told us in school to be prepared for war to break out with the Soviet Union and warned us that nuclear missiles could fall on us at any time.

We did "drills" to prepare for such an attack. We were told to hide under our little desks if the war siren sounded. Looking back on it, it sounds quite ridiculous to think that hiding under a tiny desk in a school room could save us in a nuclear explosion. But this was one fear factor that we lived with in those days. Of course, we are in much greater danger now than ever before, of a nuclear war of some sort, depending on what nation we live in.

When I was in 4th grade, while at school, the U.S. President John F. Kennedy was assassinated, and my teacher ran out of the classroom, crying.

We live in such a broken world, it is hard to picture anyone not being exposed to fearful situations, both internationally, locally, and also from the media. Although the Lord tells us not to be afraid, I often wonder how anyone can "not be afraid," amidst such dreadful dangers on every side, from the air above us, as well as our vulnerability to many dangers close to home. And for me as a child whose parents didn't know the Lord, and being frequently warned of diverse dangers, fear became frequent and inevitable.

A Death in the Family

During my entire childhood and early adolescence, my family lived next to my mother's closest relation, with his wife and children. Our families were often together, and the children always played together outside. I was the oldest of the four children. I assumed our close relatives next door shared all the same "normal" dynamics as existed in my home, regarding husband and wife, and parents towards their children.

One day when I was 12, it was a day like any other. I came home from school and went downstairs to the basement, to practice piano. Before I went downstairs, I saw that my younger cousin was waiting in the living room with my mother, because (I was told at that time) he had come home from school and his mother didn't open the door. So he naturally came over to our house. But by the time I came upstairs from practicing, he was still there on the couch, and the look on his face, and on my mother's face, indicated something was wrong. No one would tell me anything.

My father had suddenly come home early from his work in the city, but I when I came up from the basement, I learned he was out somewhere, or possibly at a hospital, with my cousin's father. I heard the mention of our family doctor's name, and I had no idea what my poor, silent, 10-year old cousin might know.

Finally, my mother told me he had come home from school and had found his mother in the garage, "sleeping" at the steering wheel, with the engine running. He probably didn't know she was dead, but he must have been terrified. Until that time, I don't think I had ever heard of anyone committing suicide, and certainly had never heard of someone using the car exhaust in a garage to deliberately end their life.

It was a frightening shock to all of us, and most especially to the deceased wife's devastated young husband, who had no idea she had taken her life out of secret love for another man. But she left a letter, which I never saw, but I was later told it explained her self-imposed despair over a sinful relationship being ended by the illicit partner. This young wife and mother had given no indications of depression, or of being involved with someone else, so the shock factor was extreme. We children were not permitted to attend the funeral, which I think was a merciful decision by the parents. None of us had ever been at a funeral before.

I cannot imagine the trauma that stayed with my cousin, who had found her this way, as well as his little sister who lost her mother but was protected from the worst details at that time. He and I stayed close for many years, but have never discussed it to this day. It leaves a mark of fear (as well as grief and anger) on any family members dealing with a suicide.

The Role of Media

In my early years, TV and movies played a huge role in my life and the lives of my parents and younger brother. Much of what we watched was innocent, especially the family TV shows, dramas, and cartoons of the '60s and into the '70s. They used to be fairly wholesome, although they were not godly, nor connected to the Lord at all.

But at least they didn't include sexual or violent content. Some had a hidden, "dark" agenda that we were not aware of, like the "magic" of Disney, comedies about "good witches," and spooky shows like "The Twilight Zone," which were very scary to me. Or the ghoulish "Adams Family," which was fixated on Death, in a "humorous way." These shows were mild, compared to the hellish depravity, horror, and violence of today's entertainment. But even back then, the seeds were sown that damaged my mental and emotional development for decades afterward. Even now, things are still being uprooted from my childhood memories.

I was a very sensitive child, compared to other children of my generation. I believe now that the Lord created me with an unusual sensitivity, which would later allow me to receive heavenly writings and songs from the Lord, and to love Him from a tender heart. But this same sensitivity would render me vulnerable to the constant flood of fearful, perverse, and violent images, which media had imprinted in my mind, and tormented almost all my nights.

My parents took me to see many movies in the movie theaters, all through my youth. Much of what they took me to see was not healthy for me, and in fact, damaged me greatly. They didn't understand how much harm these movies would do to me, lasting into my adult life, even into my latter years. Murder and horror, sinister conspiracy and psychological terror were very popular, especially in the suspenseful Alfred Hitchcock movies, which were terrifying to my young mind. I saw countless murders, and these movies deliberately manipulated the audience into sheer terror. This was entertainment, and now in today's world, it is far more graphic and destructive to young minds.

I had nightmares for many years – actually, decades, due to the onslaught of these Alfred Hitchcock movies and other terrible storylines that my parents took me to see. I lay awake in bed many nights, wondering what evil would come and attack me in my room, or attack our family in our home. I saw such terrors on the big movie screen. The successful thriller, "Jaws," about a killer shark lurking in the ocean in a holiday beach town, came out when I was about 12, and I was terrified for a long time after seeing this film. I could go on and on, but you get the idea. Fear was a major factor in what I saw on the news, watched on TV or in the movie theaters, and talked about with my parents.

My father took me (without my mother or brother) to see a movie about sexually violent criminals when I was 12, and in my complete childhood innocence, the scenes I was exposed to were beyond horrific, terrifying and confusing. I just cannot understand why he did this; probably my father didn't know the content before seeing the movie. But we all have trauma, and the Lord will heal ALL for those who cry out to Him for freedom from fear.

How vital it is for parents to guard their children, as much as is within their power, from evil media, whether online, or movies, or evil TV shows about the realm of sorcery, ghouls, vampires, zombies, and the demonic. I know that many teens don't obey their parents and manage to sneak these evil media into their phones or homes. **We reap what we sow.** And what goes into the gates of our eyes and ears are permanently imprinted in our minds. Our only hope is to be cleansed, delivered, and freed by the Spirit of the Lord, who will help us remove this filth and horror from our thoughts, our eyes, and our minds.

This is why Isaiah said, *"Depart! Go out from there; Touch no unclean thing; Go out from the midst of her, be clean, you who bear the vessels of the Lord."* (Isa.52:11).

The News

Another source of my excessive fears was the emphasis my parents placed on personal violent crimes, both inside and outside the home. I'm sure you've noticed that in a given day or week, millions of people get through with no terrible accidents or violent crimes against them or fires in their homes. But if one person or family suffers a violent crime, accident, or fire, that is what they highlight on the news, and that is what everyone is talking about. No news report tells us about the millions of people and families who got through the day safely and who woke up the next morning, very much alive.

Please keep in mind that in the generation I grew up in, there were far less violent crimes than now, and also far fewer crimes against children and teens. There were still dangerous predators in those years, but nothing like what has exploded in our culture due to the curse of internet pornography, and in particular, violent pornography. So in this generation, we actually have many more victims of violent crimes than when I was a child.

My parents were often warning me about the dangers of violent crimes, break-ins, fires, and other deadly situations. They were trying to protect me, but they watched the news on TV, and then they would warn me about whatever bad things had happened to people that day. So they feared a criminal breaking into our home and killing us in our beds, and I feared this every night. They emphasized locking the doors, which was a good thing, but the fear factor affected me almost forever.

Additionally, there were news stories of children being abducted while playing outside, or walking down the street and being found dead some time later. Of course, these terrible stories are in the news to this day, and with internet news covering the globe, they are more frequent, and the crimes more heinous than ever.

Therefore, I was taught to run away from any car that might approach me outside. This was not wrong of them to warn me, but so much fear was instilled in me, even when it was time for me to raise my own children. I ended up telling my children the same warning: run away from any car or truck that pulls up near you while you are walking or playing outside. To be honest, this is a good warning in this terrible culture, but my children teased me when they got older, for my fears and overbearing warnings. To me, it was God's mercy that they were never harmed.

Additionally, I had an immediate family member who was troubled from early childhood and became unstable and dangerous into adolescence. He threatened us. I won't detail it, but I spent more sleepless nights fearing what this person might do to us while we slept. Because we were a secular Jewish family, I don't remember either of my parents ever telling me that God could or would protect us.

There was one other bad influence from the son of my parents' close friends, who was my age, growing up. He gave me "trash" criminal fictional stories to read, which instilled in my mind new evils to fear.

The writing style of these fictional stories was bizarre. The person "telling" the story was usually a cold-blooded murderer, telling the reader his accounts, describing his crimes casually, as if he was saying, "Then I went to the store to buy milk." He had no conscience or emotions, as he described his violent deeds. Someone very sick wrote those short stories, but there I was, reading them!

You might wonder why I was willing to read this trash. First of all, I had no idea it was "trash." I only know that now, looking back on it. Also, I can tell you that with my friend's encouragement, my curiosity pulled me in. Curiosity is much more dangerous than I ever realized. I was only about 11 when this happened, and I had no idea it would affect my brain chemistry and my thought-life for years to come. I read worse things as a teenager, but we won't even talk about those.

After finding the Lord at age 19, I began to radically renew my mind and view of the world. Still, my mind would be filled with dark fears and unholy images. If only we could raise our children in the ways of the Lord at an early age, they would be spared this pollution and corruption of their minds.

Most of us were ignorant of the devilish influences bombarding our pre-teen minds. Some of us had liberal parents, who didn't know how to teach us to guard the gates of our eyes, ears, and hearts. The Lord is so merciful to forgive us and cleanse us, and even to make us holy, as He is holy. This is nothing but a miracle, with the filth I had absorbed at a young age. Praise the Lord for His grace and mercy!

The Curse of Internet Pornography

In today's advanced media, with accelerated evil agendas being propagated, what is luring the pre-teen minds now? It is so much worse than what I was exposed to. It is exponentially more dangerous, seductive, addicting and destructive of their mind and psycho-sexual chemistry. Cell phones and computers suddenly display pop-ups that imprint an instant pornographic image on their inexperienced eyes and minds. This is an image they didn't even ask to see. It found them! But that image is now "saved" in their eyes and in their minds, sometimes, till the day they die. Only the Lord can cleanse a mind from such a wicked defilement. It is embedded, but He can deliver us.

It is not only the youth who are enslaved to this fatal attraction. Millions of adults, even spiritual leaders, are addicted to some form of pornography, including violent pornography and child pornography. These ministers are deeply ashamed and keep their secret for years, even from their wives. The shame allows the enemy to keep them imprisoned in their minds of guilt.

The Lord will deliver you if you hate what this has done to you, and if you cry out to Him with ALL your heart, He will deliver you. But it will require consistent obedience and discipline on your part.

Reach out for help if you are addicted to any of these forms of evil media, involving violence, pornography, sexual deviation, or child abuse. There are ministries to help you and to keep you accountable to a trusted friend, including keeping an electronic record of what websites you have visited each day. Please repent, and get help, or it will destroy your life here, and also your eternal future. **Do not keep the enemy's secret, or he will end up having you.** Pornography is a vile idol, and the Lord will not share you with this idol. Choose this day Whom you will serve. He is strong enough to set you free.

Who may ascend into the hill of the Lord? Or who may stand in His holy place? ***He who has clean hands and a pure heart****, who has not lifted up his soul to an idol, nor sworn deceitfully* (Ps.24:3-4).

We Must Trust Only in the Lord for Protection

The Lord knows we live in an increasingly dangerous world, and He doesn't minimize how real the risks are to our safety and protection. However, His Word is full of precious promises to guard and watch over those who put their trust in Him.

I have seen His protection over my life all these years, from childhood scarlet fever and at least three severe car accidents, which could easily have been fatal. I also experienced several close encounters with a personal crime about to be perpetrated against me, but the Lord delivered me from them. In the first encounter, I didn't know the Lord yet, but He still saved me. One year after this first attempted attack, when He saved me physically, I received the Lord and He saved me spiritually. Praise His great mercy!

But I know of others who have suffered much harm, abuse, or loss, and for those who struggle, it is harder to believe that the Lord is fully protecting them. I cannot give an account for the ways of the Lord, except to say this: Throughout history, many of the Lord's most beloved children and faithful servants have suffered greatly at the hands of wicked people. This was true for the prophets of old, and for the faithful priests in His Temple; it was true for the Lord Yeshua Himself, and for all His disciples; and for millions of innocents in the years that followed, even at the hands of the so-called "Church."

We see the terror Job suffered, wondering where was God's protection and deliverance, from the great evil that Satan inflicted upon him. And this faithful man said these stunning words: *"Though He slay me, yet will I trust Him."*

So we can conclude this chapter by saying that **trust is the opposite of fear**. We can feel afraid for good reasons. But trusting God is a deliberate choice we must make: One fear at a time, one decision at a time, day by day, fear by fear, and faith by faith. Amen.

Chapter 3
The Many Meanings of "Fear"

You will not fear the terror by night
Nor the arrow that flies by day
Nor of the pestilence that stalks in darkness
Nor the destruction that lays waste at noonday.
Psalm 91:5-6

The Hebrew word for "fear" is *"yar'eh."* Strong's Concordance (H3372) defines *"yar'eh"* as: "to fear, revere, to be afraid; to stand in awe, reverence, and respect." The majority of biblical uses mean: "**to fear**," and "**to be afraid**."

In another form of the verb, it means, "to be dreadful, fearful, terrible."

This word is also used as a noun, i.e., "the fear of the Lord" (*yir'at Adonai*). This principle also occurs in English. The English word "fear" is also both a noun and a verb, as we see in these examples:

"I struggle with **fear**." (noun)
"He **fears** that his teacher will fail him in Science." (verb)

When we do a word search for *yar'eh*, we find an almost uncountable number of times it appears throughout the Hebrew Old Testament. We also see it in the New Testament, in its Greek form *(phobos)*. Let's look at two examples.

Anytime you come across this word, it will generally be:

a. Referring to fearing human enemies, armies, or any predatory thing, e.g., "Israel **feared** the Philistines." Or, "The people of Jericho **feared** Joshua and the Israelites."

b. Referring to fearing the Lord Himself; honoring and deeply respecting Him, out of reverent fear for His sovereignty and power. For example, "You shall **fear** the Lord your God and serve Him." Or, "Cornelius was a **God-fearing** man."

If We Fear the Lord, Are We Afraid of Him?

We must understand the context, each time this Hebrew word is used in Scripture. It most often means **fear**, with the exact same meaning as our English word, **fear**. Some Bible interpreters only present the idea of "respect or reverence," when referring to the biblical phrase, "the fear of the Lord."

This teaching is correct, to a degree, and it is understandable why they minimize the idea of "being afraid of God," because He is a loving God. They don't want people to be afraid of this loving God. But if we don't balance this with the full counsel of Scripture, we could end up with error, in either direction.

To walk in the complete truth of this complex doctrine, we must go deeper. As we study Scripture, we will see three distinct contexts in which this word is used. Depending on the context, we will understand what kind of fear the Lord is referring to. Here are the three contexts:

1. To **fear,** to **be afraid** of, or to **dread** people or enemies: those who might be a threat to our life, position, safety, respect, finances, or to our family's well-being. To fear diseases, wars, random disasters, famine – anything or anyone that could harm us or others we care about. **Both believers and unbelievers** can experience this first aspect of **fear.**

2. To fear the **Lord Himself**, to walk in the Fear of the Lord, **from the position of being one of His own**, His chosen and saved people, whether from Old or New Testament times. To show **reverence** for the Lord and to fear Him with this clean and healthy motive: **Fearing we might insult, disobey, displease, dishonor, or disappoint Him.** This good motive should *not usually* include the "Fear of Punishment."

2a. However, this is not an absolute rule, that we should not fear punishment. There are biblical exceptions to this point, and there are solid, biblical reasons to fear God's punishment. In the Gospels, the Lord emphasized both eternal rewards and eternal punishment. So we must be balanced. **The Lord Yeshua Himself told us to fear the One who could inflict the punishment of Hell** (see Lk.12:4, Mt.10:28). We will cover this issue fully in Chapter 8, "The Fear of the Lord."

Here is the main point so that we won't be confused: **This reverential, loving Fear of the Lord is truly the BEST motive for obeying.** When you love Someone, you don't want to hurt Him. That is the best possible motive.

2b. Nevertheless, if a person is a rebel, and bent on disobedience, it is far better that they fear the eternal punishment of hell, than not to fear God at all.

However, the Lord does not want His people to fear His punishment. He wants them to love Him and fear Him, but from a heart of knowing His goodness and kindness, not His harshness and punishment.

3. To fear the Lord Himself, but NOT from a position of being one of His own people.
This context is referring to the enemies of God Himself, who are dreading (and then experiencing) His wrath, vengeance, plagues and ultimately, eternal torment. An example would be the fear Pharaoh felt, as he and his charioteers saw the walls of the Red Sea begin to crash down around them. Too late, he realized the God of Moses was fighting against them. This God was treating them as His own enemies. Another example is how His enemies will feel on the Great and Terrible Day of the Lord.

> *I looked when He opened the sixth seal, and behold, there was a great earthquake; and the sun became black as sackcloth of hair, and the moon became like blood. And the stars of heaven fell to the earth, as a fig tree drops its late figs when it is shaken by a mighty wind.*
>
> *Then the sky receded as a scroll when it is rolled up, and every mountain and island was moved out of its place. And the **kings of the earth**, the great men, the rich men, the commanders, the mighty men, every slave and every free man, **hid themselves** in the caves and in the rocks of the mountain, and said to the mountains and rocks, **"Fall on us and hide us from the face of Him who sits on the throne and from the wrath of the Lamb. For the great day of His wrath has come, and who is able to stand?"*** (Rev.6:12-17).

Let us think about the relationship between the **Fear of the Lord** and **obtaining mercy**. In doing so, we will be contrasting the points made in **Numbers 2** and **3** listed above.

Number 2 is about the Fear of the Lord that **leads to favor, mercy,** and **rewards**.

Number 3 is about the Fear of the Lord that comes in the midst of **punishment, wrath,** and **irrevocable judgment**.

Most of us, as we read our Bibles, are not conscious of these three different interpretations of the exact same word: FEAR. If we think about these three contexts, we will know what is meant by the word "fear" in a given passage of Scripture. It doesn't always mean exactly the same emotion, in all its diverse usages.

There is even a fourth aspect of the Fear of the Lord, which is not included in the three cases above. I will cover this in Chapter 9: "The Judgment Seat of Messiah." This is a different judgment, for believers only. This type of fear will affect those who were counted among the saved, but who were not prepared to meet the Lord, for a number of biblical reasons. These believers will fear the Lord in a painfully regretful way, but there is still the element of mercy in these cases. It is not the same as undiluted wrath.

Even believers who are prepared for that Day will also fear the Lord when they see Him as Judge. However, the Lord's response to their love, preparedness and obedience will make the fear easier to bear, and without regrets. The theme of Chapter 9 will be that we do not want to suffer **any** regrets on that Day. If we have regrets in this life, we can repent, talk with the Lord, obtain mercy, and do better the next time. But on that Day, there is no chance to do better or to change the Lord's evaluation. This is healthy fear.

"I Knew You Were a Harsh Man"

A good example of discerning the context of **fear** in a given passage is found in Luke 19:11-26, "The Parable of the Ten Minas."

Here is a brief summary of the opening section of this parable: Before going away on a long trip to receive a kingdom, a certain nobleman gave a sum of money (one mina) to each of his servants, expecting them to invest it in some way, during His absence. One mina was about three months' wages at that time, quite a lot of money.

After He returned from this journey, He called the servants, asking them for an accounting of the money. The first servant gave his mina back to Him, along with a tremendous gain of interest. The second servant also gave the Master a large increase, though not as large as the first. The Master was pleased with both of them, who had both invested His money profitably while He was away.

But the third servant only gave Him back the original mina with no interest, having hidden it away during his long absence. Let's look at the reason/excuse given by this third servant: He was too "afraid" of the Master to invest it!

Then another came, saying, "Master, here is your mina, which I have kept put away in a handkerchief. ***For I feared you, because you are an***

austere man. *You collect what you did not deposit, and reap what you did not sow."*

And he said to him, "Out of your own mouth I will judge you, you wicked servant. ***You knew that I was an austere man,*** *collecting what I did not deposit and reaping what I did not sow.* ***Why then did you not put my money in the bank****, that at my coming I might have collected it with interest?"*(Lk.19:20-23).

The Greek word for "austere" is *"austeros,"* and Strong's Concordance gives this definition: "of harsh, rough, rigid mind and manners."

It is important that we rightly interpret this parable, which has always puzzled and troubled me. In my own personal fear of the risk factors, I could relate to the third servant being afraid to invest the money, for fear of losing it altogether. However, not all investments carry much risk; some are very stable and safe, under normal circumstances. Since the Lord had no sympathy for the servant who didn't invest it at all, we can assume that in the context of this story, there were safe investments readily available, while the Master was away.

As the Heart Believes, the Lord Responds

Let's look at the heart attitudes of these three servants. The Master was well pleased with the first two, who were rewarded with authority over many cities, proportionate to their respective gains. Each of them had taken the effort to find safe investments, and had invested their Master's money and gained excellent returns. Although the first servant gained more than the second, the Master was equally happy with both of them, but the one who gained more received a larger reward.

Here's the key: What was their motive for moving forward and investing it? Both of them respected their Master and wanted to **honor** and **please Him**, by giving Him a well-deserved return on His investment. This is where the words, "honor, reverence, and respect" apply to the word **"to fear"** the Lord.

They also wanted to make Him glad and wanted Him to know they highly esteemed Him. They valued the fact that He trusted them with His money. Each of them did their best to gain what they could for the Master.

Now, let us carefully examine the heart motives and thoughts of the third servant, who greatly displeased the Master. Even the little he had been entrusted with was taken away from him.

"For I feared you, because you are an austere man. You collect what you did not deposit, and reap what you did not sow."

Now notice the first part of the Master's angry reply.

"You knew that I was an austere man, collecting what I did not deposit and reaping what I did not sow."

Please notice that the Master **does not deny** that He is a hard (or harsh) man. He seems almost to acknowledge that He is a hard man. Why does He not deny it? Is He truly a hard man?

No. In fact, He is not, but this is one of the most intriguing paradoxes about the Lord's personality, and what it means to **fear** and **revere** the Lord. His decisions and behavior are often a **reflection** of our own decisions and behavior. Isn't this remarkable? We see this principle all through the Scriptures, from Old to New Testament, even to the very end.

Here is an example from the Psalms, since King David knew the Lord's heart better than anyone in his generation.

With the merciful You will show Yourself merciful; with a blameless man You will show Yourself blameless; with the pure You will show Yourself pure; and with the devious You will show Yourself shrewd (Ps.18:25-26).

David understood that when a person has a noble, merciful, and pure heart towards Him, the Lord responds in like manner. He treats that person with the same purity and gentleness with which that person treats Him. But with the devious or perverse person, the Lord shows Himself clever, shrewd and adversarial. He uses their own words against them. Their own words will judge them!

*"You **knew** that I was an austere man, collecting what I did not deposit and reaping what I did not sow...**out of your own mouth I will judge you**, you wicked servant."*

The Lord did not admit He was an austere man. Rather, He said, "You **knew** I was austere." The Lord actually meant this:

"Your opinion of Me was harsh. You considered Me to be unkind, unfair, punishing, and greedy for others to do work I wasn't willing to do Myself. Therefore, I will treat you exactly as you imagine Me to be, even though you have misjudged Me. If you **knew** I was hard, I will, therefore, treat you **with the very harshness you expected of Me.**

"You have not esteemed Me, but have thought the worst about My character, and thus, you were 'afraid' I would be harsh with you if that one mina went missing. If you had honored and esteemed Me and had truly feared and revered the Lord, I would have honored and esteemed you, as I did My other faithful servants, who esteemed and revered ("feared") Me."

We will look at a few more Scriptures that help support this understanding:

As in water face reflects face, so a man's heart reveals the man (Prov.27:9).

When we look at our reflection in the water, we can never see anything other than our own exact face. In the same manner, whatever is in a man's heart reflects the character and motives of the man.

The Lord saw the motives of the third servant, who was afraid of His Master's harshness. He was the one who judged the Master harshly, believing the worst about the character and motives of his financially successful Master. This false judgment in him manifested as an unhealthy **fear of punishment** from a Master inclined to be unfair.

The Lord does not feel honored or loved when someone's motive for obedience is fear of punishment. It is important for all of us to check our motives whenever we feel afraid of the Lord. If we are afraid of punishment, it is not honoring to Him. What honors Him the most is fearing to hurt His heart, fearing to let Him down, fearing to inadvertently insult Him, or to diminish His kindness in any way.

Our Reverent Fear of the Lord Attracts His Heart

Here is an incident where the Lord heals, on the basis of the faith and reverence of two blind men:

And when He had come into the house, the blind men came to Him. And Jesus said to them, "Do you believe that I am able to do this?"

They said to Him, "Yes, Lord."

Then He touched their eyes, saying, "According to your faith let it be to you." And their eyes were opened. And Jesus sternly warned them, saying, "See that no one knows it" (Mt. 9:28-30).

We see that these two blind men honored the Lord, believing He was not only **able** to do this but that He was **willing** to do this. They knew His heart was kind, and according to their understanding of His character and their faith, it was done for them.

But why does He then add, *"See that no one knows it."*?

Is it only His humility, or His fear of greater crowds thronging Him? I believe it is because this healing was granted **on the basis of their faith**, and the Lord was responding, according to what was in their hearts. Is it possible that someone with a different attitude might not have received the same miracle?

There are many Scriptures that support this possibility. Let's look at three examples of this principle. In the Lord's own hometown of Nazareth, He did not do many miracles, due to the disrespectful and offended hearts in this place.

When He had come to His own country, He taught them in their synagogue, so that they were astonished and said, "Where did this Man get this wisdom and these mighty works? Is this not the carpenter's son? Is not His mother called Mary? And His brothers James, Joses, Simon, and Judas? And His sisters, are they not all with us? Where then did this Man get all these things?" **So they were offended at Him.**

But Jesus said to them, "A prophet is not without honor except in his own country and in his own house" (Mt.13:53-57).

Now **He could do no mighty work there,** *except that He laid His hands on a few sick people and healed them. And He marveled because of their unbelief* (Mk.6:5-6).

In our next example, please pay attention to what this sick and bleeding woman was thinking in her heart, just before the Lord's power healed her, even before He saw who she was.

And suddenly, a woman who had a flow of blood for twelve years came from behind and touched the hem of His garment. **For she said to herself, "If only I may touch His garment, I shall be made well."** *But Jesus turned around, and when He saw her He said, "Be of good cheer, daughter;* **your faith has made you well.**" *And the woman was made well from that hour* (Mt.9:20-22).

This woman revered (feared) and honored the Lord. She knew virtue and healing radiated out of even the edge of His garments. This is a good example of "reverently fearing the Lord," but **not being afraid** to touch Him. If she had thought He was "a harsh man," she would have been too afraid to touch Him. But she trusted in His kind motives.

Our last example is found in the account of the paralytic healing at the Pool of Bethesda.

After this there was a feast of the Jews, and Jesus went up to Jerusalem. Now there is in Jerusalem by the Sheep Gate a pool, which is called in Hebrew, Bethesda, having five porches. **In these lay a great**

multitude of sick people*, blind, lame, paralyzed, waiting for the moving of the water... **Now a certain man was there who had an infirmity thirty-eight years***. (Jn.5:1-3,5).

Notice that a great multitude of sick people lay at the pool that day. They all trusted in the Angel that stirred the water and were waiting for their miracle. **The Lord only healed one man at the pool that day.** He could have healed all of them, but He was directed by the Father to only heal this one. We don't know if something in this man's heart caught the Lord's eye and moved His heart. We do know that the Lord is never random or unintentional in any of His choices. There was something about that man that drew the Lord to him alone. Perhaps it was an unusual level of the Fear of the Lord in his heart.

In conclusion, returning to the healing of the two blind men in Matthew 9, the Lord had said, *"See that no one knows it."*

The Lord never made widespread announcements of instant and universal healing. In fact, He often warned those He had healed **not** to spread the news, as we saw in this case and many others. The Lord knew the miracles were dependent on the will of the Father, **and on the attitudes of the ones being healed.**

He is always looking at our hearts. Amen.

Chapter 4
Do Not Fear Them – I AM With You!

God is our refuge and strength, a very present help in trouble
Therefore we will not fear, even though the earth be removed
And though the mountains be carried into the midst of the sea
Though its waters roar and be troubled.
Psalm 46:1-3

In this chapter, we will study the biblical references to the Lord commanding His people not to fear nations, enemies, and dangers. Through this study, we will learn the Lord's remedies for fear, but it is not a simple formula. Rather, it is an intimate knowledge of the Lord's loving heart and His purposes for our lives. These cases show us how to interact with the Lord during threatening situations in our lives, and also how to rely on Him during more "normal" times.

Let's begin with some samples in the Bible, which all carry a similar remedy for fear. After each passage, I will highlight the **command** NOT to fear, and then I'll highlight the **reason** God gave them WHY they shouldn't fear.

1. *And they turned and went up by the way to Bashan. So Og king of Bashan went out against them, he and all his people, to battle at Edrei. Then the Lord said to Moses, **"Do not fear him, for I have delivered him into your hand**, with all his people and his land* (Num.21:33-34).

Command: Do not fear this king.
Reason: God has already delivered him into their hand.

2. *And I said to you, 'You have come to the mountains of the Amorites, which the **Lord our God is giving us**. Look, **the Lord your God has set the land before you**; go up and possess it, as the Lord God of your fathers has spoken to you; **do not fear or be discouraged'** (Deut.1:20-22).

Command: Do not fear or be discouraged.
Reason: The Lord is giving us the land, and He has set the land before us.

3. *"And I commanded Joshua at that time, saying, '**Your eyes have seen** all that the Lord your God has done to these two kings; so will the Lord do to all the kingdoms through which you pass. **You must not fear them, for the Lord your God Himself fights for you**'* (Deut.3:21-23).

Command: You must not fear them.
Reason: You have seen how the Lord has destroyed the others; now, the Lord Himself fights <u>for you</u>.

4. *Be strong and of good courage, **do not fear nor be afraid of them**; for the Lord your God, He is the One who goes with you. **He will not leave you nor forsake you*** (Deut. 31:6).

Command: Do not fear or be afraid of them.
Reason: He goes with you, and He will not leave you or forsake you.

How Can We Walk in This Same Confidence?

In the examples above, the Lord is not standing far off, impassively, and seeing His people face impossible situations. He is not just watching to see how they will handle it. As a younger believer, I used to think the Lord was just observing how I handled fearful and painful situations but was not intervening for me in a tangible way. In really rough times, I even thought He didn't care about my problems, because mine were not as terrible as other people's problems. This was wrong thinking that partly stemmed from my secular upbringing. The truth is that the Lord has always been **more** involved than we realize. It takes faith to believe it.

When the Lord tells us not to be afraid, He also gives us the understanding that He has gone ahead of us and is with us. Whenever the Israelites were embarking on a **Kingdom assignment,** given directly from the Lord (conquering the Promised Land), He had already ordained their victory. He was fighting for them and would not forsake them. But they still had to fight.

Therefore, in order to know He is fighting for us, we too must be intentional about pursuing **His assignments**, those which He ordained for us to do. We must be about our Father's business. Thus, He will not let us fight the battles alone, but will stay close to us and help us.

What is a "Kingdom Assignment?"

Before we examine our own lives and discover our assignments, let's return to David as our role model. He knew the Lord's people were being threatened by the Philistines and that the Lord wanted to deliver them. David knew of the Lord's past deliverance from various enemies in the days of Joshua and the judges.

David realized that Goliath (and actually all the Philistines for years to come) was not just a physical threat, but he was a haughty mocker. His goal was to humiliate the God of Israel and His armies, proving that their God could not save them from the Philistines' superior military strength or the superiority of their false gods.

David could discern when **God's reputation** as the Lord of Hosts (Heaven's Armies) was at stake. Therefore, every time David fought the Philistines, he was on a Kingdom Assignment to defend the honor and reputation of the God of Israel, as well as to physically deliver Israel's troops.

David thought in a covenantal way, in a **Kingdom mindset.** He understood from Scripture the Lord's perspective of Israel's destiny. David had received his original commissioning from the prophet Samuel, and this gave him the confidence to go into Kingdom battles. He also had two prophets that the Lord appointed to him: Nathan and Gad. With their help, David was able to accurately discern his kingdom assignments. On one occasion, David consulted the priest to discern God's will for him, in a desperately dangerous situation (see 1Sam.23:9 and 30:7). We too will need to understand God's eternal covenants and His purposes for our generation, in order to have the confidence to go boldly into our assignments.

We also must discover His specific assignments for each of our individual lives on this earth. We must know our own destinies, chosen by the Lord for us. (This topic will be covered in Chapter 7.)

Over the course of his life, David suffered many trials, threats, wars, and great discouragement. Not every season in his life was like his original victory over Goliath and the Philistines. That was only one moment in his life. But as we read the Psalms, we see his fears exposed, and we learn of his spiritual weapons for overcoming fear.

David's Battles

There is so much we can learn from David, who had to fight not only outward battles but inward battles in his own soul. He bares his heart in the Psalms, encouraging us all to rise up in faith and to see the Lord helping us in each situation. In this way, we learn to overcome our fears. I'm convinced he wrote the Psalms for us, not only for himself.

But You, O Lord, are *a shield for me, my glory and the One who lifts up my head...I lay down and slept; I awoke, for the Lord sustained me.* ***I will not fear ten thousands of people*** *who have set themselves against me all around* (Ps.3:3,5-6).

When David was running for his life, he was constantly finding new hiding places, fearing being caught like a hunted animal. Each night when he lay down to sleep, he didn't know if he would wake up the next morning. There was a real possibility Saul's spies would track him down and murder him in his sleep. Could you sleep peacefully under these conditions?

The Lord was a shield to him, though His protection was not visible to the natural eye. The Lord was his glory (honor and defense) and the One who lifted up his head above his circumstances and his enemies.

This is why he said, *"I awoke, for the Lord sustained me."* He knew he only got through each night safely by the Lord's sustaining power. David was a real man who dealt with His fears by knowing the Lord's love and commitment to sustain him in times of threat.

Yea, though I walk through the valley of the shadow of death, ***I will fear no evil****; For You are with me; Your rod and Your staff, they comfort me.* (Ps.23:4).

There were long periods when David was constantly in danger of sudden death. He had to keep going and not let this terror suffocate him. At times, his governmental and military aids, trusted friends and even his own sons, betrayed him and sought his death. He didn't know where to turn or who to trust, and the shadow of death hung over him.

How could he fear no evil? *"Lord, You are my Shepherd. Your rod and Your staff comfort me."* The rod and staff indicate a loving shepherd, guiding, prodding, and directing the sheep away from danger. David saw God as His shepherd, always keeping him safe, despite unparalleled dangers to his life.

This is a tool for us, this understanding of the Lord as the Good Shepherd, which also our Lord Yeshua displayed so magnificently in His care of His own flock, during His years on earth. Yeshua also continues, even now in His resurrected glory, to manifest His role as the Good Shepherd in His gentle, yet firm leadership of His entire flock across the earth. We depend on His shepherd-like guidance and protection every day of our lives, as David did, and He performs this task perfectly from His heavenly vantage point.

*The Lord is my light and my salvation; whom shall I fear? The Lord is the strength of my life; of whom shall I be afraid?....**though an army may encamp against me, my heart shall not fear;** though war may rise against me, in this **I will be confident**.* (Ps.27:1-3).

The Lord was David's light (guidance), salvation (deliverance) and strength (both outward and inward strength). In Hebrew, the word "salvation" (*"yeshuah"*) does not only mean the saving of our eternal souls after death. This word means "physical deliverance and rescue." Even when powerful armies surrounded him, the Lord was his physical salvation and the strength of David's life. He put no confidence in his own ability to deliver himself. Can we say the same of our lives and protection?

*For I hear the slander of many; **fear is on every side**; while they take counsel together against me, **they scheme to take away my life**.* (Ps.31:13).

He was surrounded by intrigue and traitors on every side. How could he trust anyone?

*I sought the Lord, and He heard me, and **delivered me from all my fears*** (Ps.34:4).

Only by going through fiery trials and seeing the Lord take us through to the other side, will we be able to give this same testimony as David.

*Therefore **we will not fear**, even though the earth be removed, and though the mountains be carried into the midst of the sea* (Ps.46:2).

In our current time, we will face geological upheaval in the earth, the seas, flares from the sun, and other distressing signs. Our Lord spoke plainly about these coming events and told us not to fear, just as the psalmist tells us we will not fear. Only God can give us His peace and trust in these coming atmospheric and geological disruptions, even when the mountains shake.

Why should I fear in the days of evil, *when the iniquity at my heels surrounds me? (Ps. 49:5).*

Hated and hunted, surrounded on every side of his mountain hideaways, David chooses not to fear.

Fearfulness and trembling have come upon me, and ***horror has overwhelmed me****...Hear my voice, O God, in my meditation;* ***preserve my life from fear of the enemy****.* (Ps.55:5, 64:1).

He has known paralyzing terror, in circumstances where he has lost all hope of escaping with his life. He confesses to God, and also to all who will read his psalms, that he has despaired even of life. And yet, time and time again, David says to his soul: *"Put your hope in God"* (Ps.42:5,11).

The Apostle Paul also wrote about being in such peril that he despaired, even of life:
For we do not want you to be ignorant, brethren, of ***our trouble*** *which came to us in Asia: that we were* ***burdened beyond measure****, above strength, so that* ***we despaired even of life*** (2Cor.1:8).

We can take courage from Paul, David, and the other psalmists' words, showing that they were weak flesh, just as we are. But they **overcame fear through the intimate knowledge** of their mighty Lord and His mercy. They knew He would help them in their distress. May we do likewise, and through faith and courage, may we receive the Overcomer's Crown (see 1Cor.9:25, Rev.2:10).

Mercy Triumphs Over Fear

Our God has so many attributes, but there is one quality by which He defines Himself. This quality is **part of His Name**; it is how God defines God.

In Hebrew, someone's name is **who they are**; it is their character. Hebrew names have meaning, e.g., *"Judah"* means "praised," and *"Benjamin"* means, "son of my right hand."

This quality is one of the Lord's kindest responses to our **fear**. No matter what we fear – whether enemies, sickness or death, poverty, loss, or betrayal – there is **one word** that rings out 276 times throughout Scripture. David and the other Levitical Psalmists sang about this beautiful quality exactly 100 times in the Psalms!

And even these numbers do not come close to the number of times each one of us has received the comfort of this blessed attribute: HIS MERCY.

The Lord God presented Himself to Moses, proclaiming **His Name** (character, attributes). This is how He wanted Israel to know Him:

*Now the Lord descended in the cloud and stood with him there, and **proclaimed the Name of the Lord.** And the Lord passed before him and proclaimed, "The **Lord,** the **Lord God,** **merciful** and **gracious,** **longsuffering,** and **abounding in goodness and truth*** (Ex.34:5-6).

This is the merciful One whom we are privileged to love and serve. The Lord's mercy is seen in the lives of virtually all our biblical forefathers.

Joseph was unjustly sold into Egypt by his jealous brothers. Later, he was falsely accused by his master's seductive wife and thrown into prison, where he remained for many years. In prison, Joseph cried out to the Lord, who was His only help, his only hope.

*But the Lord was with Joseph and **showed him mercy,** and He gave him favor in the sight of the keeper of the prison* (Gen.39:21).

As we know, the Lord continued to show Joseph greater and greater mercy, until He exalted him to become the Savior of Egypt and of his father's family – and of the fledgling nation of Israel.

We see David, continually contending with fear and in trouble so many times. He shares with us his vulnerable cries for mercy and deliverance. He declares and extolls the Lord's mercy uncountable times.

Have mercy on me, O Lord! *Consider my trouble **from those who hate me,** You who lift me up from the **gates of death*** (Ps.9:13).

Surely goodness and mercy shall follow me *all the days of my life; and I will dwell in the house of the Lord forever* (Ps.23:6).

*I will be glad and **rejoice in Your mercy,** for You have **considered my trouble;** You have **known my soul in adversities*** (Ps.31:7).

*He shall send from heaven and **save me**; He reproaches the one who would swallow me up. **God shall send forth His mercy** and **His truth*** (Ps.57:3).

When I've been in overwhelming danger, sickness, fear, or grief, I have often cried out to the Lord for mercy. Whether I sinned, or someone else sinned – when my situation became too much to bear, I cried out for mercy.

This is a prayer the Lord will not ignore. If His children will come humbly and cry out for mercy, He will move to the sound of our voice. He has proven faithful, despite many griefs and sorrows. **Mercy is one of God's keys for overcoming Fear.**

I will now share with you one severe trial in my life, where I was overwhelmed with sorrow and fear, and even despaired of life.

My Terrible Test

Like most of us, I have been through hard, perplexing, and agonizing situations throughout my life. This world is badly broken, and as teacher Neville Johnson wisely said, "You cannot get through this life unscathed."

However, he also shares that every trial in our life has been permitted by the Lord to test us, try us, and refine us in the fire so that our faith will emerge as gold.

But He knows the way that I take; when He has tested me, I shall come forth as gold (Job 23:10).

Even though the enemy afflicted Job, the Lord had granted permission for him to be sifted, as He also did when the enemy demanded to sift Peter. After the test, Job came out as gold, and the Lord restored all that the enemy had stolen. And Peter was beautifully restored, after his most severe test and failure. Peter wrote about the glory of coming through the fire.

*In this you greatly rejoice, though now for a little while, if need be, **you have been grieved by various trials**, that the **genuineness of your faith**, being much **more precious than gold** that perishes, **though it is tested by fire**, may be found **to praise, honor, and glory** at the revelation of Jesus Christ, whom having not seen you love. Though now you do not see Him, yet believing, you rejoice with joy inexpressible and full of glory, receiving the **end** (meaning, <u>goal</u> or <u>culmination</u>,) of your faith—the salvation of your souls.* (1Pet.1:6-9).

Some years ago, I was suddenly immersed in a shocking and devastating trap, one which I never considered or prepared for. It happened while I was alone in a hotel in Asia, after having finished a successful and intense ministry trip in this particular nation. It was still three days before my flight to the next country where I would minister, and I had free time in the hotel for those days.

I am not at liberty to share all the details, but I will share what I can. Nothing physically happened to me in that hotel; I was perfectly safe, physically. However, there was a breach of my email communication, which happened accidentally, while I was trying to fulfill the request of a fellow minister, via email. Neither this request nor the fellow minister had anything to do with the crisis that followed.

There was an email from the past, which contained a prophetic word that a prophet had spoken over my life several years before. It was a word that had troubled me greatly, and I was not able to discern if it was an accurate word from the Lord or not. The prophet was a trustworthy person, but it was hard to believe the Lord would have said this. I was torn over this for years, for it carried conflicting and disturbing implications. I still do not have the wisdom to know whether the Lord spoke it or not.

All at once, far away from my hotel room, this email was accidentally intercepted by someone close to my life, and it caused an irreversible chain of reactions, which seemed to threaten the fabric of my life, my family and closest ministry partners. The email did not reveal any sin in my life, but it made me falsely appear to be aligned with an ethically questionable prophetic word that someone else had spoken.

The person who accidentally found it severely misunderstood the email and felt betrayed. I was judged harshly and was cut off in an instant. I couldn't reach them by phone or email for several days, and I was devastated. Deprived of communication, I had no one but the Lord to turn to.

I thought my life was over, as well as my ministry, and the enemy made sure I **knew** my life was over and that I would never recover from this ruin. The enemy told me that suicide was the only way out of this, and I briefly thought about it. I had to fight that terrible thought and temptation, which I knew was not from the Lord. Thankfully, I knew better than to consider it further. David spoke of this horror.

Fearfulness and trembling have come upon me, and **horror has overwhelmed me** (Ps.55:5).

All that day, I lay on my face on the floor of the hotel room, crying and begging the Lord for mercy. I didn't eat but eventually drank tea. The next day, it was still impossible to reach this person, though I left messages and emails. That day, too, I lay on my face, crying out to the Lord. I only drank a couple of cups of tea. On the third day, I heard back from the person, who was now at least talking to me, though clearly all trust was shattered. But I was so relieved that at least we had a brief conversation. That third night at midnight was my flight out to the next nation, where I was to minister six times in one conference, beginning the day I landed.

The Shadow of Death

I was dropped off late at night at this third-world airport and was left there alone. I hadn't eaten in 3 days, and I was depleted, stressed, and still frightened of the consequences of this terrible disclosure. I didn't realize what a serious toll the stress and fear of this trauma had taken on my health. As I waited for my midnight flight, surrounded by throngs of people, I began to feel symptoms of a heart attack in my chest. It wasn't sharp pain, but it felt like I had a golf ball in my esophagus. I was sweating and light-headed. I knew I had eaten nothing, so there could not be any food in my esophagus. I bought a bottle of water and was drinking it, as I began pacing the floor, praying in tongues and quietly rebuking a heart attack, while the people watched. I know I looked like a crazy American woman, but I was more afraid of dying on the flight out, than what they thought of me. I tried to call an intercessor on my U.S. cell phone, but the call couldn't go through.

I thought seriously about telling the authorities I was not well and that I was having symptoms of a heart attack. However, nothing in me wanted to do that. I knew if I told them, they would not let me board my flight, and they would take me involuntarily to a hospital. A hospital in a third-world nation did not sound like a safe thing to do.

I was alone and wasn't sure I could reach the ministry that had been hosting me, who had dropped me off at the airport. I had never communicated with them on my cell phone. Apart from them, I knew no one, nor did I speak the language. Even if I reached them, they would have called an ambulance or told the airport authorities. In either case, I would never get to the next nation, where I was the keynote speaker, and they were waiting for me.

I decided to trust the Lord. I knew it was possible I would die on the 4-hour flight, but I felt it was better to try to get to my next assignment than to be dragged off to a hospital alone in this nation.

I said to the Lord, "At least You will know I tried to go to Your assignment for me. If I die, at least I tried."

I suddenly saw that people were already boarding my flight! I hadn't noticed, due to my emergency. I got in the back of a long line, barely able to stand up. A stranger offered me a place in line, right near the front. He didn't even know I was sick. I know that was from the Lord.

Then when I got on the plane, they looked at my card and said I had been upgraded to business class! I was shocked, but I knew it was the Lord taking care of me. When I got into business class, they offered me orange juice, and I gladly drank it. I had wanted to keep fasting till I got to my destination, but I felt my body needed the juice. I rested peacefully and prayed during the flight.

By the time we reached the destination, I felt completely normal. No golf ball, no sickness. Just normal. The Lord delivered me because I trusted in Him. I know the enemy wanted to take me out, even if it only meant getting me stuck in a foreign hospital and missing the entire ministry trip.

When I met my hosts in the other country, it was early morning, and we all went to a restaurant in the airport and had a wonderful breakfast and great conversation. I was meeting these folks for the first time. I spoke all my scheduled slots at the conference, had an unplanned meeting with an esteemed minister that changed my life, and it was the most glorious ministry trip ever! I also ended up meeting a new sister there, who would later become one of the greatest blessings of my life, along with her family.

He sent from above**, He took me; He drew me out of many waters. **He delivered me from my strong enemy, from those who hated me,** for they were too strong for me....the Lord was my support. He also brought me out into a broad place; **He delivered me because He delighted in me.

You have also given me the shield of Your salvation; ***Your right hand has held me up, and Your gentleness has made me great*** (Ps.18:16-19, 35).

Mercy!

When I finally returned home about a week later, the Lord showed me mercy. He restored all my relationships to me, and it became as if nothing had happened, within days of getting home. I was still troubled, but those who had been angry and hurt realized I had done nothing to betray them or anyone else.

During this fiery trial, I had to overcome horrendous fear, when I thought my life was over. The fear that gripped me was flooding my body with panic for three full days and nights, and filling my mind with desperate thoughts. But I needed to move forward into what **I knew were the Lord's assignments for me**. Therefore, He fought *for me, not against me*. He fought this battle for me because I was on His assignment and trying to do His will. And because I put my trust in Him alone to save me.

As for the prophetic word spoken years before – well, that will remain in the Lord's hands. It isn't something I have any control over, anyway. I will keep serving the Lord, and He will do what is His perfect will for my life if I remain in obedience and faith.

Sometimes, we don't get clear answers to the most perplexing and painful questions. This terrible case is one of them, but it gives us a chance to trust Him in the darkness, for He is full of grace and truth.

Will He Fight Our Battles?

If we need the Lord to fight our battles, it is vital that **His battles become our battles** and not the other way around. We cannot just decide to do whatever we want, go wherever we want, or pursue our own goals while presuming on the Lord's approval, support, and protection. Of course, He is always with us and will never leave us. But that is not the same as the Lord intervening to fight for us with supernatural strength and strategies we would not have on our own.

How can we know if the Lord will send Heaven's armies to fight with us and for us, as He did for Moses, Joshua and for David? They were following His plan. They were executing His will. They were fighting His battles and thus, He fought with them and for them.

Let us press in, and we will closely examine our lives and priorities before the Lord. In doing so, we will discover our unique Kingdom assignments, and how to walk in the destiny He has prepared for each of us before we were born. **Knowing His assignments,** as did our biblical forefathers and mothers, **is another one of God's keys to overcoming fear.**

When we know we are doing His perfect will in our lives, we will also know He has gone ahead of us and will deliver us from all our fears. In Chapter 7, we will explore how to discover each of our destinies. Amen.

Chapter 5
Worry and Anxiety

There is no fear in love, but perfect love casts out fear
Because fear involves torment
But he who fears has not been made perfect in love.
1 John 4:18

Up until this point, we've been speaking of fear as a strong, negative, emotional, and chemical response to a threatening situation. In the Bible, it often involves a threat to life or livelihood, through persecution, judgments, or calamity. This powerful and damaging emotion is experienced by both believers and unbelievers.

In the last chapter, I shared my testimony of a severe crisis suddenly falling upon me, through email, while in a lonely, third-world hotel room. I tried to convey to you how intense was my fear of ruin and desolation. I felt my life was completely and permanently destroyed, as well as my closest relationships, on which I depended heavily.

It's true that I wasn't in mortal danger. Except that the fear and stress of this event could have caused me a heart attack. At that point, in the airport, making that life-and-death decision as to whether to get on the plane, my fear was partly for my physical survival, and partly for the ruins of my life and ministry that awaited me at home (or so I thought.) The chemistry of fear is dangerous to our health, as any doctor will confirm.

But what about "worry" and "anxious thoughts?" Is "worry" the same thing as these intense fears we've been discussing? Or is it a different area of our soul to overcome?

Distinguishing Between Fear and Worry

The Bible has many instructions regarding worry, anxiety, and the cares of this life and the world's systems. Just as the Lord told us repeatedly, *"Do not fear,"* He also tells us in several ways, *"Do not worry or be anxious. Your Father will take care of you."*

He shares with us the dangers of being distracted, weighed down, and occupied with the needs and cares of this life. Worry is a type of fear, but it is more continual, like a low-level, destructive emotion under the surface, and much less intense than fear. You could say that "worry" is indulging in the lowest level of fear, without admitting we are afraid.

*Therefore I say to you, **do not worry** about your life, what you will eat or what you will drink; nor about your body, what you will put on. Is not life more than food and the body more than clothing?* (Mt.6:25).

The Lord assures us that our necessities are known by our Father and that we don't need to waste our energy, worrying ahead of time about how we will get our needs met. Does this stop us from worrying? It should, but in most cases, we do not obey this particular instruction. I know He already knows what I need. Why do I worry about it, then? It must be a lack of trust that causes me to keep worrying (on and off).

*Now he who received seed among the thorns is he who hears the word, but **the cares of this world** and the **deceitfulness of riches** choke the word, and **he becomes unfruitful*** (Mt. 13:22).

The Lord warns us not to be distracted by the cares of this world, including the deceitful temptation of gaining riches, or the obsessive fear of losing them. Whether we gain them or lose them, we must leave it in the Lord's hands. He compares these worries to thorns that suffocate the green plant, preventing it from bearing fruit. Thus, we will be without Kingdom fruit, if we are distracted in this way.

He also tells us that not only will we be unfruitful, but that we will also be **unprepared for the Day of the Lord:**

*"But take heed to yourselves, lest your hearts be **weighed down** with carousing, drunkenness, and **cares of this life**, and that Day come on you unexpectedly"* (Lk.21:34).

And the Lord adds this awesome instruction, which will protect us on that Day:

*"For it will **come as a snare** on all those who dwell on the face of the whole earth. **Watch** therefore, **and pray** always that you **may be counted worthy to escape** all these things that will come to pass, and to stand before the Son of Man"* (vs.35-36).

The Lord instructs us that the **remedy** to being weighed down by the cares of this life is to **watch** and **pray**. To "watch" means to remain vigilant and prophetically aware of the times in which we live. To recognize the signs of His soon coming is also part of "watching." The reward of watching and praying, instead of worrying, is to be counted **worthy to escape** the snare and deception that is coming and to stand before Him without shame or regret. In the next chapter, we will cover the biblical way to understand the season, age, or epoch of biblical history, in which we live.

Even in Persecution, <u>Do Not Worry</u> about Defending Yourself

The Lord is honest with His people, letting us know we will be persecuted. He knows it is natural for us to worry about how we will defend ourselves when brought before an unrighteous judge. Our very life is dependent on how we answer our accusers. Or is it?

*You will be brought before governors and kings for My sake, as a testimony to them and to the Gentiles. But when they deliver you up, **do not worry about how or what you should speak. For it will be given to you** in that hour **what you should speak** for it is not you who speak, but the Spirit of your Father who speaks in you.* (Mt.10:18-20).

We must always remember this instruction, if and when we are brought before rulers who might be considering harsh punishments for us. The Holy Spirit will fill our mouth with what HE wants us to say. But this does not guarantee that His words in our mouth will cause the rulers to show mercy to us.

The Lord Yeshua Himself only said what the Father told Him to say, but even though He spoke the Father's Words to the spiritual leaders of the Jewish people, they ultimately delivered Him over to the Roman torture and crucifixion.

Likewise, in Acts 7:1-53, Stephen is brought before the Sanhedrin and told to give a defense for what he believes. He gives the most awesome summation of Israel's founding, history and deliverance from Egypt.

He also summarizes Israel's unbelief in the days of Moses and of the prophets. Stephen spoke all these words by the Holy Spirit. It was all an accurate accounting, but suddenly, he exposed the very generation he was addressing. He accused them of having committed the same unbelief and killing of the prophets as their ancestors; they had murdered "the Righteous One," meaning the Lord Yeshua.

As soon as Stephen reached that climax of accusing them of what they had truly done, they rejected his words and immediately dragged him out to be stoned. Even though Stephen's inspired speech was completely led by the Spirit, the result was that he was martyred and not delivered.

I share this to give us perspective so that even if we don't worry ahead about what we will say, it does not ensure that we will be set free. The Lord permitted Stephen to be martyred and his death was a precious seed in the earth, for the later salvation of Saul of Tarsus, who was there, giving approval to Stephen's death.

Be Anxious for Nothing

Both the Old and New Testaments admonish us not to worry or be anxious, nor to carry heavy cares and mental burdens on our souls. The Lord Himself spoke the most gracious and peaceful words to us, inviting us to place our burdens on His shoulders. There is nothing like this gentle passage to tenderize our hearts enough to lay down our worries and burdens. Amen?

"Come to Me, all you who labor and are heavy laden, and I will give you rest. Take My yoke upon you and learn from Me, for I am gentle and lowly in heart, and **you will find rest for your souls.** *For My yoke is easy and My burden is light"* (Mt.11:28-30).

The Apostles Peter and Paul also remind us of how much the Good Shepherd cares about our anxieties and burdens.

Therefore humble yourselves under the mighty hand of God, that He may exalt you in due time, **casting all your care upon Him, for He cares for you** (1Pet.5:6-7).

Be anxious for nothing, *but in everything by prayer and supplication, with thanksgiving, let your requests be made known to God; and* **the peace of God**, *which surpasses all understanding,* **will guard your hearts** *and minds through Christ Jesus* (Php.4:6-7).

Anxiety in the heart of man causes depression, *but a good word makes it glad* (Prov. 12:25).

King Solomon has given us the last instruction about anxiety – it causes depression! May we all take it to heart, and once and for all, rid our lives of worry, anxiety, stress, and fear.

This is a decision each of us must make, day by day, choice by choice. The Scriptures have clearly warned us about the **dangers, depression, and distraction** that affect us when we let financial or worldly worries and cares grip our hearts.

I too struggle very much with worry, but I pray that as we meditate on these urgent messages, even from the Lord Himself, that we will discipline our minds, hearts, and emotions, to be aligned the Lord's heart. May He set us free, as we make every effort to obey His Word. He will help us to walk in His peace.

My Dream

As I was just finishing writing this book, I had a dream that might have been about worry. I came back to the end this chapter, and have now added this new revelation. In the dream, I looked down into the ground and saw a large, neatly dug-out open grave, without any coffin filling its large space. The space was nearly empty. However, I saw many white, rectangular cards, lying in the bottom of the grave. Each white card was about two-feet wide and about 8 inches high. All were identical, and all had two words neatly typed in the center of the card: **"What If?"**

Then I saw someone's arm holding a shovel, and the shovel began to scoop up and remove piles of these cards and lay them on the grass outside the grave. The shovel was just taking piles out and putting them somewhere else. I woke up.

As I pondered the meaning, I felt that my constant worrying about everything that could possibly go wrong, was like a grave full of "What If's?"

What if I forget some critical governmental or banking responsibility? What if that document gets lost in the mail, or the Fed Ex plane crashes with my irreplaceable document? What if I forget to do vital tasks that are on my plate? What if someone I love is killed or disabled suddenly? What if certain technical aspects of our home fail, and there is no way to get them fixed, where I live? What if I don't have enough money for all the ministry flights and shipments coming up?

I also thought about some other more serious worries that I cannot write openly in this book, but they are real issues that could destroy aspects of my life and destiny. I worry constantly about these threats, and they are many.

I realized I am often playing every negative scenario, with the words, "What if?" running in my brain. I wasn't conscious of this until I had the dream.

Then, when I was awake and talking to the Lord, I felt like He wanted me to take those words out of the grave of death and destruction, and into the Land of the living. I started speaking these good "What If's?"

"What if I can bring comfort to many?"

"What if I can speak, pray, and prophesy the truth?"

"What if I can help His bride to walk into their destiny, get into His heart, walk closer with Him?"

"What if I can help the poor and oppressed, to lift up the desperate?"

"What if I can do lasting works for His Kingdom?"

The Lord wants me to change my thinking and take it out of the grave. I think the Lord wants us to change our expectations, from negative possibilities that lead to death, into positive and wonderful possibilities that will lead to new hope and life for many. We can all put our own "What If's" into our heart and into our mouth, and see if it changes our propensity to worry.

Amen.

Chapter 6
Who is On the Lord's Side?

*Those who trust in the Lord are like Mount Zion
Which cannot be moved, but abides forever.
Psalm 125:1*

Let's think about our own lives. I know we are not living in the days of Joshua, nor of David. We are not living in ancient Israel, surrounded by cruel nations, seeking to devour us. However, it is incredible to realize that modern Israel is definitely living in a hostile, powerfully-armed Middle East, surrounded by cruel, merciless nations who seek their destruction. Even in our "safe" countries, there are real threats from other nations.

If we had time in this book, we could examine a number of factors and see that we are in a remarkably similar situation to our heroes of old. So things are not quite as different as you might think, between ancient Israel's Kingdom assignments, (along with threats from enemies who outnumbered them), and this generation's Kingdom mandates, (along with severe dangers of massive, global proportions).

But whether times and circumstances are different or similar, one thing we know: **Our God is the same, yesterday, today and forever.** He never changes, and His commitment to keeping His covenant responsibilities to His own ones has never wavered for an instant. Halleluiah!

Where is God's Story Going?

The Bible is a historic storyline, told by Creator God. It is God's story, from His perspective. Since He is the One who created the Heavens and the earth – and it is He who created Time itself, He is the only One who has the full and accurate perspective on the timeline of His story. Stories have beginnings and endings, and the Bible also has a beginning and an ending. However, His Kingdom is an everlasting Kingdom, and His reign will have no end.

But the Lord speaks often in His Word about seasons and ages, both beginning and ending. It would be too long a Bible study to document this point. But as we look through Bible history, we see different epochs and ages, where dramatic **transitions** take place, but they don't happen in one instant. They happen gradually over time, and yet for those with eyes to see and ears to hear, the changes are monumental, and everything shifts to a new reality. It is wisdom for us to understand our times and to know where we fit in, and why we were placed here at this time.

All believers in the Lord are called to know and follow their callings, no matter what generation they are born into. For every person in every generation, there is a purpose for which the Lord placed them on the earth. But it is even more critical to know our calling if we are living in a transitional generation, where circumstances and culture as we know them are experiencing rapid and dynamic change. Time seems to be speeding up as we draw closer to the Lord's return. I am convinced we are living in a transitional generation, and we cannot afford to miss the calling and purposes of the Lord for our life.

We will now study four cases of this principle of **transitional generations**: two from the Old Testament; one from the New Testament period; and one from the End of the Age.

1. Israel at Mt. Sinai

One of the greatest transitions in human history was that of the fledgling nation of Israel coming out of 400 years of slavery in Egypt. The Lord dramatically freed them from their slave status and through the leadership of Moses, led them out into freedom. They were in the early stages of becoming a new nation. They were required to enter a Covenant with the Lord, the invisible and eternal God. This covenant included loyal love, exclusive worship of the Lord, and obedience to His laws.

Their forefathers had known this relationship with the Lord, and their own parents would have taught them about Abraham, Isaac, and Jacob. But after 400 years in Egypt, they could easily slip back into a pagan mindset and its idolatrous worship system.

While Moses was on the mountain for many days, receiving these laws from the Lord, the people reverted to the dependency on physical objects (idols) to worship. They were like children, and without Moses' physical presence to comfort and instruct them, they became **fearful**. They had no leader anymore (or so they thought.) They didn't know how to worship the true God and began to demand an image to worship, as they had seen in the Egyptian religious system.

> *Now when the people saw that Moses delayed coming down from the mountain, the people gathered together to Aaron, and said to him,* **"Come, make us gods that shall go before us;** *for as for this Moses, the man who brought us up out of the land of Egypt, we do not know what has become of him."*
>
> *And Aaron said to them, "Break off the golden earrings which are in the ears of your wives, your sons, and your daughters, and bring them to me."... And he received the gold ... and made a molded calf.*
>
> *Then they said, "This is your god, O Israel, that brought you out of the land of Egypt!"*
>
> *So when Aaron saw it, he built an altar before it...and the people sat down to eat and drink, and rose up to play.*
>
> *Now when Moses saw that the people were unrestrained...then* **Moses stood in the entrance of the camp, and said, <u>"Whoever is on the Lord's side—come to me!"</u>** *And all the sons of Levi gathered themselves together to him* (Ex. 32:1-6, 25-26).

In this crucial transition, the new nation of Israel was divided. Those who clung to the security of idols turned against the Lord. Moses asked one question of them: **"Who is on the Lord's side?"**

Only the Levites chose the Lord over idolatry. They chose to put their trust in Him, rather than letting fear drive them to trust in worthless idols. In every generation, the Lord is seeking those worshipers who understand His requirements and are willing to fearlessly carry them out. Those who have chosen His side.

2. Saul and David

Now there was a long war between the house of Saul and the house of David. But David grew stronger and stronger, and the house of Saul grew weaker and weaker (2Sam.3:1).

In this passage above, we see that the Lord was **transitioning a generation of leadership,** from Saul's dynasty to David's. This change didn't happen overnight, but it was a season of transition. In those days, if God's people understood the Lord's purposes and knew what the Lord was doing (i.e., strengthening the House of David and weakening the House of Saul,) they would rightly align themselves with David before the transition was complete. Otherwise, they might be caught in the wrong loyalties later, and that would have put them in a dangerous position.

Before we move to the next example, we need to see something critically important here:
- If a believer who lived during that long transition between Saul and David, did not rightly discern the times and seasons of God, he might wrongly align himself with the House of Saul, thinking he was honoring God's anointed king. He might have excellent theology to defend his behavior. But the truth is, he would miss the day of the Lord's visitation, and the Lord would not protect him from the consequences of having missed the Lord's transition. It could even have cost him his life.

3. The Transition of Jerusalem's Fall

Another enormous transition in God's storyline occurred during the Lord Yeshua's ministry on earth. His public ministry was a short 3.5 years, but events of unimaginable significance took place during the Days of the Son on earth, and in the generation following His death and resurrection.

The Lord honored and loved Jerusalem, calling her "the City of the Great King" (see Mt.5:35, Ps.48:2). As a child and youth, He came up to Jerusalem regularly with His family, to worship the Lord and honor His Feasts. We also see that He was drawn to spend time in the Temple, discussing the Scriptures with the learned teachers and leaders of that time (see Lk. 2:49).

About 40 years after His death and resurrection, a horrific calamity came upon the Lord's city, Jerusalem. The history of the long Roman occupation, as well as the Jewish resistance and revolt against Rome that led up to this catastrophe, is a massive subject. It is not our purpose to cover this history, but only to study this calamity in view of understanding transitional times – **the ending of an age and the beginning of another**.

The putting down of the Jewish revolt finally culminated in a long siege, starvation, and ultimately, the destruction of Jerusalem and the burning of the Temple in 70 A.D., at the hands of the enraged Roman army under Titus. Hundreds of thousands of Jews were killed and also a massive number enslaved, which resulted in the premature and cruel deaths of the slaves as well.

As we mentioned, the Lord Yeshua's ministry on earth took place 40 years before this calamity would take place. The Lord prophesied it would happen, shortly before His death. He also gave the reason why it would happen, which is chilling, but noteworthy.

In His final entry to Jerusalem, just days before His cruel and unjust death, the Lord could not hold back His grief any longer; He looked out over the city He loved and pronounced these agonizing words, with many tears:

Now as He drew near, ***He saw the city and wept over it****, saying, "If you had known, even you, especially in this your day, the things that make for your peace! But now they are hidden from your eyes. For days will come upon you when your enemies will build an embankment around you, surround you and close you in on every side, and **level you, and your children within you, to the ground**; and they will **not leave in you one stone upon another**, because you did not know the time of your visitation"* (Lk.19:41-44).

The Wrong Side of History

Let's look at this phrase: *"...You did not know the time of your visitation."* The Lord was not speaking to individuals in Jerusalem but was speaking to the city itself, and primarily, **to the spiritual leadership of that city** (the Sanhedrin).

He knew that a significant number of the common people had loved Him and had received great miracles from His healing hands. There were also at least two Pharisees who believed in Him, named Joseph of Arimathea (see Mt.27:57) and Nicodemus (see Jn.3:1-2). There were other Pharisees who secretly believed in Him, but couldn't face the persecution that would have come if they confessed it (see Jn.12:42). It is even possible that several Sadducees secretly believed in Him, though we cannot be sure.

The Lord was aware of the cruelty and suffering that would ensue, and He wept for His city. He prophetically saw the future destruction, anguish and uncountable deaths of helpless families, weak and unarmed civilians, young children, the elderly, and pregnant women. As He trudged up the hill to His agonizing crucifixion, He saw the daughters of Jerusalem mourning and weeping for Him along the way, for they knew He was a righteous and innocent Man. He looked at them kindly and spoke prophetically to them.

But Jesus, turning to them, said, "Daughters of Jerusalem, do not weep for Me, but weep for yourselves and for your children. For indeed the days are coming in which they will say, 'Blessed are the barren wombs that never bore, and breasts which never nursed!' Then they will begin to say to the mountains, 'Fall on us!' and to the hills, 'Cover us!'" (Lk.23:28-30).

He wasn't thinking of Himself. He knew it would be so terrible, that the people would wish they had never given birth and nursed their babies, compared to seeing your children being slaughtered, starved or crucified in such an inhumane and torturous manner.

But who did not recognize the day of their visitation? **Who got on the wrong side of history? The wrong side of biblical prophecy? <u>Who was not on the Lord's side?</u>**

The Lord prophesied judgment to the **spiritual leadership** of the City of the Great King. They had taken the wrong side, the wrong position, the wrong assessment of the One whom the Father sent to the city He loves.

We must not be arrogant against those Jewish spiritual leaders, who missed the day of their visitation and unknowingly brought such calamitous judgment to His own chosen people, and even to His Holy Temple. Could a believer in this generation also take the wrong side? Could we misunderstand the signs of our times, and not recognize where we stand on the Lord's timeline? Could we unknowingly align with false doctrine?

If we do not recognize and align ourselves with the Lord's purposes in this generation, He will not fight for us either, as He did not fight for Jerusalem in that terrible hour. Paul cautions the Gentile believers not to think they are immune to the same consequences if they do not stand firmly with the Lord's heart and purposes.

You will say then, "Branches were broken off that I might be grafted in. Well said. Because of unbelief they were broken off, and you stand by faith. Do not be haughty, but fear. **For if God did not spare the natural branches, He may not spare you either.** *Therefore, consider the goodness and severity of God: on those who fell, severity; but toward you, goodness, if you continue in His goodness. Otherwise you also will be cut off* (Rom.11:19-22).

The Lord has chosen Jerusalem, and yet He did not save her in 70 A.D. It changed the course of Israel's history and the course of Jewish history. It was a transitional time, leading to the scattering of the Jews to the four corners of the earth. This also led to astonishing fulfillment of biblical prophecy in the latter years, in which we now live. That, of course, is another topic, which is covered in my book, "Israel's Prophetic Destiny."

Theirs was the transitional generation, on whom the destiny of Jerusalem hung, and they got it wrong. <u>May we never be so blind, for we are not immune to spiritual blindness and deception, such as that which</u>

came upon the leadership of that generation. Let us keep our hearts humble and low so that we might not be deceived.

We want the Lord to fight for us in the day of trouble, just as He fought for Joshua, David, and Jehoshaphat. He also fought for Daniel in the lion's den, and the three young Hebrews in the furnace. He fought for Mordechai and Esther because they were aligned with His purposes for that generation. He fought for the Apostle Paul, though he suffered so much. Still, the Lord was with him in every trial, and His grace was sufficient for Paul. The Lord stood with Paul as he fought the lions and delivered him from shipwreck so that he could testify before Caesar.

*But the Lord stood with me and strengthened me, so that the message might be preached fully through me, and that all the Gentiles might hear. Also **I was delivered out of the mouth of the lion*** (2Tim.4:17).

*If, in the manner of men, **I have fought with beasts at Ephesus**, what advantage is it to me? If the dead do not rise, "Let us eat and drink, for tomorrow we die!"* (1Cor.15:32).

...Saying, 'Do not be afraid, Paul; you must be brought before Caesar; and indeed God has granted you all those who sail with you.' (Acts 27:24).

If the Lord is fighting for us and has gone ahead of us, **we will not fear**. If we are aligned with His Kingdom destinies, He will fight for us, and we will be delivered.

[**One more special note**: I understand that some of us are appointed to martyrdom, by the will of the Father. Please know that His grace will be as strong to carry us through that destiny, as it will be for those whom He physically saves from their persecutors. His help and grace are with us in all cases. Amen.]

4. The Kingdom of our Lord

Now let's look at our fourth example of transitioning kingdoms, found in the Book of Revelation. This scene takes place just as the Lord Yeshua the Messiah is returning to establish His reign over all the kingdoms and nations of the world. We see this transition from one kingdom to another so clearly, it is unmistakable.

Then the seventh angel sounded:

And there were loud voices in Heaven saying, **"The kingdoms of this world have become the kingdoms of our Lord and of His Christ, and He shall reign forever and ever!"** [Transition #1 - From the world's ungodly governments and leadership to the leadership of King Yeshua, the Messiah, and Lord of all the earth.]

And the twenty-four elders who sat before God on their thrones fell on their faces and worshiped God, saying:

"We give You thanks, O Lord God Almighty, the One who is and who was and who is to come, because **You have taken Your great power and reigned**. [Transition #2 - From the age of corrupt human rulers to the righteous government of the Son of David.]

"The nations were angry, and **Your wrath has come**, [Transition #3 - From the age of grace and forbearance to the Kingdom Age of Justice and Righteous Judgment]

"And **the time of the dead, that they should be judged** [Transition #4 - From the age where the dead bodies laid in the ground indefinitely, to the time when the Lord raises the dead in Christ, and they come and stand before His Judgment Seat, to be evaluated, and to receive their rewards]

"And that You should **reward Your servants the prophets and the saints, and those who fear Your name**, *small and great,* **and should destroy those who destroy the earth."** [Transition #5 - From the age when the righteous and innocent were not rewarded, and the wicked did what was evil, and were not punished, to the age when the righteous are rewarded, and the wrath of the Lamb is poured out upon the wicked, whose punishment has been stored up for this hour.] (Rev.11:15-18).

Are Our Spiritual Leaders Missing the Day of Our Visitation?

In the five transitions above, it is critical that we understand the transitional generation in which we live. If we do not rightly discern this transition, **we will not be prepared** for the unprecedented events that will come to Israel and to the nations.

I have heard teachers say that the Lord will not return for at least 100 more years. Other leaders are saying He will not literally return *at all*, because Jesus is already reigning from Heaven, and He doesn't need to return to reign on earth.

But wait! Didn't Yeshua **say** He was returning? To the very Mount of Olives from which He ascended? But now someone decided, "He doesn't need to return?"

They do not believe the end of this age will bring a literal *thousand-year Kingdom of Yeshua* over the earth, reigning from Jerusalem, as the greater King David. The word *"Millennium"* means "one-thousand years" in Latin.

Those who deny a literal, future Millennium believe we are *already living in the Millennial reign of Messiah now*. How can that be? They interpret the "Millennium" as a figurative, indefinite length of time, not as a literal thousand-year period. They view all of history, ever since the resurrection of Yeshua, as a continuing *spiritual "Millennium,"* with the Lord reigning from Heaven.

This doctrine is called *"Amillennialism,"* meaning, "there is no literal thousand-year reign of Yeshua in the future." In Latin, the prefix *"A"* means *"without."* Thus, *"Amillennial"* means *"without a Millennium yet to come."*

However, chapters 19 and 20 of Revelation reveal the return of the Lord as a conquering King. We see Him coming in zeal and power, leading the armies of heaven. John plainly tells us we will reign with Him for a thousand years.

They lived (came alive) and **reigned with Christ for a thousand years***...they shall be priests of God and of Christ, and shall reign with Him a thousand years* (Rev.20:4-6).

This chapter cannot teach this subject in-depth, due to the quantity of biblical support needed. I have fully documented the biblical case for a literal Millennium in the Appendix at the end of this book. My main point for this chapter is that if we do not recognize the transition from this age to the Kingdom age, we will not be prepared for the upheaval preceding the Lord's return, nor for the establishment of His Kingdom. It will affect the way we prepare our hearts now; we will be unprepared if we do not understand the signs of the times.

*If you would like more historical background on the doctrine of *Amillennialism*, and more biblical evidence for a Pre-Millennial and literal understanding of the Lord's return, please see the Appendix at the end of this book.*

The Mark of the Beast

Following this pattern of denying or spiritualizing the biblically prophesied events preceding the Lord's return, some are teaching that there will not be a literal "mark of the beast." They have a more figurative understanding, viewing "the mark" as a mindset; a mental and emotional dependence on worldly financial systems for our safety and security. They say "the mark" is only figurative, a way of thinking wrongly, but not literal. Not something that will be physically imposed upon the hands and foreheads of all people. *The Bible says otherwise.*

It is true that if believers are trusting in the world's systems – financial networks, credit cards, cellular data transmission, and other technology – they will be easy targets for an electronic ID or other devices that would no longer be a plastic card or a cell phone, but would now be implanted under the skin. Most of us are attached to the systems of the world. We find our security in our financial access, medical and pharmaceutical access, and the ability to transact business.

Our mindset is critical for our inward preparation, but we cannot deny the biblical, literal, end-time realities. If we spiritualize "the mark," **we will not be prepared to say "no,"** when the realities – the snare, the trap, the fatal test of our loyalty to God – are thrust upon us. We might allow a bio-chip, or a vaccine injection/chip, or a cellular communication (phone) implant, or a bank-card chip/implant to be placed under our skin because we think it couldn't possibly be "the mark." But Beloved: **What if it is the mark?** Once you accept it, there will be no turning back (see Rev.13:16-18).

Please remember the words of our Lord:

*"For it will **come as a snare** on all those who dwell on the face of the whole earth. **Watch** therefore, **and pray** always that you **may be counted worthy to escape** all these things that will come to pass, and to stand before the Son of Man"* (Lk.21:35-36).

Worthy to escape what? If we **watch** and **pray**, we will be **counted worthy to escape** the **terrible trap, snare, and deception that is coming**, and to stand before Him without shame or regret.

The Rapture

One other biblical truth that has also been "spiritualized" by certain Christian leaders is the reality of the Rapture, as Paul taught in 1Thess.4:16-17. They have interpreted the meaning of the Greek word, translated "<u>caught up</u>," and have replaced its literal meaning with a figurative meaning. Let's examine the actual Greek New Testament text to demonstrate the literal meaning of this word.

For the Lord Himself will descend from heaven with a shout, with the voice of an archangel, and with the trumpet of God. And the dead in

*Christ will rise first. Then we who are alive and remain **shall be <u>caught up</u> together with them <u>in the clouds</u>** to meet the Lord <u>**in the air**</u>. And thus we shall always be with the Lord* (1Thess.4:16-17).

The Greek word for "caught up" used by Paul is "*harpazo*," pronounced "har-pad'-zo." The King James Bible translates Strong's G726 like this: **To catch up; take by force; catch away; pluck; catch; pull.**

Its biblical usage is: "to seize, carry off by force; to seize on, claim for one's self eagerly."

This Greek word is derived from G138, meaning: "to seize, pluck, pull, take (by force)."

Does this sound figurative to you? Or was Paul describing a literal catching away of the people of God? Just reading the true Greek definitions should settle this issue. Scripture clearly teaches a literal rapture, though we don't know the timing of this event. We must prepare ourselves to endure until He comes (see Rev. 13:10).

Agreeing with the Lord's Judgments

Even though we fear the judgments of the Lord, we must stand in agreement with His righteous judgments, as we see in the passage below. His wrath is not directed at His children or His bride. It is directed at the enemies of God and the tormentors of His people.

*They sing **the song of Moses**, the servant of God, and the **song of the Lamb**, saying: "Great and marvelous are Your works, Lord God Almighty! **Just and true are Your ways, O King of the saints!*** (Rev.15:3)

In this heavenly Song of Moses and Song of the Lamb, the overcoming saints rejoice at the Lord's righteous judgments. They stand in agreement that He is a God of justice and truth. None would dare to call Him "rash" or "quick to judge." He has been long-suffering for thousands of years, restraining Himself and waiting for men to come to repentance. We will agree with all His ways, even in judgment. This song is like the rejoicing of Moses and the Israelites when they saw the Lord's judgment on Pharaoh's troops.

The Lord knows the end from the beginning. He desires that we too, as His bride, share His perspective on "where this is going." He wants us to partner with Him in the unfolding and fulfilling of all He has purposed for this generation.

I believe we are in a transitional period, from this present age to the Kingdom Age. As the Lord's time on earth was nearly over, His disciples asked Him about the timing and the signs of the "end of the age."

Are We Living at the End of the Age?

Where are we on that timeline? Many have theories and theologies, but we will only present what we see clearly in the Word of God. The Lord gives us signs that precede His coming and the end of the age.

Now as He sat on the Mount of Olives, the disciples came to Him privately, saying, "Tell us, when will these things be? ***And what will be the sign of Your coming, and of the end of the age?****"* (Mt.24:3).

And Jesus answered and said to them: "Take heed that no one deceives you. For many will come in My name, saying, 'I am the Christ,' ***and will deceive many.*** *And you will hear of* ***wars and rumors of wars.*** *See that you are not troubled; for all these things must come to pass, but the end is not yet. For* ***nation*** *("ethnos")* ***will rise against nation*** *("ethnos,") and* ***kingdom against kingdom.*** *And there will be* ***famines, pestilences, and earthquakes*** *in various places. All these are the beginning of* <u>***sorrows.***</u> (Mt.24:4-8).

The Greek word for "nation" is *"ethnos,"* and Strong's Concordance (G1484) defines it this way: "Probably from G1486; **a race,** a tribe; especially a foreign (non-Jewish) tribe." The usage is that of a Gentile, heathen, nation, or people.

The Greek word for "sorrows" is *"odin,"* and Strong's Concordance (G5604) defines it this way: "Sorrow, pain, travail…akin to G3601, meaning, 'the pain of childbirth, travail, birth pangs.'"

The Lord compares this Kingdom transition to a woman travailing in childbirth, with the pains coming closer and with greater intensity as she nears the birth. He describes racial and tribal violence increasing, as the term *"ethnos"* denotes, as well as international conflicts intensifying.

It is evident that we are living in a time when these signs are happening before our eyes. Deception and false doctrines have increased and are luring professing believers into apostasy. True prophetic voices have noted a number of unparalleled "advancements" in the realms of science, genetic engineering, artificial intelligence, astronomy, and demonic technology. It is not within the scope of this book to explore the dangers and evils of using advanced science to tamper with the human genome, to clone humans, to create artificial or robotic life, or to attempt to communicate with "aliens" and their advanced technologies. These evils and the mixing of the seeds of life (DNA) are reminiscent of the days of Noah. Mankind is attempting to replace God as creator, and it will bring judgment, as it did in the days of Noah. Daniel tells us that knowledge will vastly increase.

*But you, Daniel, shut up the words, and seal the book **until the time of the end**; many shall run to and fro, and **knowledge shall increase*** (Dan.12:4).

In addition to these, we see an exponential increase in blasphemy, cruelty, pornography, lying media, satanic worship, theft, murder, inconceivable abuse of children, and moral degeneracy. These are a few signs which verify that we are living in the times Yeshua described in Matthew 24, and which Paul described in 2 Timothy 3:1-9. I believe the Lord's return is sooner than we think. We must prepare our minds and hearts for unprecedented upheavals in our nations, in the earth, in the weather, and in the unraveling of law and order.

Time seems to be accelerating, heading for a volatile transition from this age to the Kingdom age. As the birth pains increase in magnitude and in frequency, we need to seek the Lord's wisdom to interpret the times in which we live. Our nations will become unstable, and it will be a fearful time. But – **no fear for His people!** He will still be with us, closer than our heartbeat.

The Lord spoke of persecution, tribulation, and betrayal in these treacherous days. At the same time, false prophets will be deceiving people, and false Messiahs so convincing, that even His own chosen ones could be deceived if it were possible (see Mt.24:15-25). Let us watch and pray, so we will not be unprepared for disruptions, deceptions, and distress among the nations.

The Lord is taking history to a destination; a goal; a fulfillment; a KINGDOM, made without human hands, as Daniel was shown (see Dan.2:34-35, 44-45).

We Must Know Our Assignments

The Lord had specific kingdom assignments for Abraham, Moses, Joshua, David, Elijah, and so many others in Bible history. He designed each of their callings to prepare the earth for the greatest Kingdom transition of all time: the First Coming of the Lord Yeshua the Messiah, who would become the Atoning Sacrifice for all sins ever committed, to those who would avail themselves (receive Him and His sacrifice for the atonement and forgiveness of their sins).

The Lord has also placed His appointed servants in every generation, who took the gospel to the nations, and did extraordinary exploits even in the darkest places, the cruelest institutions, the most repressive governments, and the most hostile climates and conditions.

In the same way, **the Lord has also prepared unique kingdom purposes for each of us**, in this generation, to prepare the earth for the next greatest event on the prophetic calendar: the Return of the Lord Yeshua the Messiah to the earth, as He promised us He would come.

We each have a calling from the Lord, and we need to find out what He has ordained for us, and how we can walk in this calling. These assignments are precious, chosen just for us, and are necessary for the Lord's full plan to be accomplished.

Often, our calling was placed within us at a young age, but for many years, we only had the slightest sense of what we were meant to become. Even before we were saved, the Lord had already deposited **seeds of destiny** within us, though we hardly realized it.

As we grow older, the Lord will use many factors around us and inside of us, to nudge us toward the calling He has placed in us. Some have dreams, and most of us have at least one natural gifting or feel pulled strongly in a certain direction. However, the Lord's thoughts and plans for you may be quite different than what you would have guessed, based on your natural strengths.

Many have a range of gifts, but their destiny assignment might only require one small portion of their gifts, or His assignment might use almost all their natural gifts. Or the Lord will give them surprising new gifts to match their new destiny work. Some discover their calling late in life. Even so, with diligence, they can make up for all those lost years and will run their race for the crown set before them. At times, these will excel even the ones who were running their race from an earlier age.

Just as the Lord brought history to a climax in the birth, ministry, death, and resurrection of the Lord Yeshua the Messiah, so He is now, in these last days, bringing history to another climax, which will culminate in the Return of our Lord.

This time, He is not coming as a sacrificed Lamb for the sins of the world. Rather, He is coming as the Conquering King, the Righteous Messiah, marching in the zeal of His strength, with all Heaven's Armies (see Isa.63, Rev.19). He is coming to judge the nations, to take up His Throne (Seat of Government), and to establish His Millennial Kingdom over the earth. There is much work needed to prepare for His coming, even more than the preparation that was needed for His first coming.

John the Baptist (the Immerser) was just one man, preparing Israel to meet her Messiah, the Lamb of God, through repentance. But in the last days, there will be a vast company of forerunners, whom the Lord will send to prepare not only Israel but all the nations, for the return of the King.

Do not minimize the vital role you've been assigned in this cosmic drama between the Kingdom of God and the kingdom of Satan. The Lord has appointed destiny assignments for every one of us. We were born for such a time as this. **We all have a tailor-made calling to fulfill in His storyline!** This is not a time for the mundane, for plodding through our work and life, with no wisdom or insight as to the brevity of time before the Lord returns. We cannot afford to be unprepared and caught off guard.

Do Secular Jobs/Professions Conflict with God's Will?

The Lord's plans for us, even His perfect will for us, will not usually rule out the normal need to work "regular jobs," or to be at home as caregivers to children or aged parents. Working a normal job in the workplace does not disqualify anyone from being in God's will. Walking in obedience does not usually involve quitting our jobs unless the Holy Spirit clearly directs us. Most people have to work for a living, and that is part of life.

Some believers are specifically called by the Lord to come out of the worldly system of financial provision and to serve the Lord "full time." This can only be determined by the Lord's plans for each individual life, not by human rules. The Lord is the only One who can show you His plans for your life.

I worked regular jobs much of my life, as a believer and a mother raising three children. There were some years I taught in Christian schools, so my children could attend these schools with free tuition.

In my current stage of life, the Lord has called me out into His assignments, which take time, strength, and resolve. I love the work He has given me because it fits me perfectly, but it requires discipline. The Lord has also asked me to travel, teach, and minister in diverse places, so there is an element of sacrifice and hardship in the travels.

Some of you reading this book are currently working in full-time ministry, such as pastors, evangelists, worship leaders, or missionaries. If Lord Himself has called you to do this ministry work, then you are obeying Him and walking out His Kingdom assignments.

However, there are some in ministry who cannot honestly say that the Lord called them into this work. They may have ended up in some type of Christian ministry, and the Lord may have blessed it, but that does not mean that the Lord initiated it. Only you and the Lord can answer this question. He will show you if any change needs to be made. I know several beloved ministers, who shared how they had prepared for years to be missionaries, but then the Lord intervened and told them they had a different calling altogether. Or He changed their destiny later in their life. For example, they were already serving in missions, but then the Lord called them to be a pastor, or a prophet, or the director of a satellite TV station!

Using our Time Wisely

Our obedience to the Lord is also expressed in how we spend our free time when we are not at work, and how we use the money that God has given us. What do we allow our eyes to see and our ears to hear, and what do our mouths speak? Remember that the "gates" of our body are our eyes, ears, and lips. Do we guard our gates, as to what flows in and out of us? What entertainment do we permit to come into our hearts and homes, our bookshelves and computers? Where are our priorities in the use of our time when we are not at work or doing the normal, necessary things?

Is entertainment our god? I see this endless distraction stealing people's destinies all the time. And I too struggle with the pull of the easy path of doing something "entertaining," rather than the discipline of prayer, fasting, waiting on the Lord, or reading the Bible. We have choices every day. Usually, there is an easy choice and then there is the Lord's choice. It is easier to be entertained than to wait on God. We'll never get that time back!

Remember, He is looking at our heart, our loyalties and our motivations, whether in the workplace, in ministry, or at home doing house-related work. It is our heart and our obedience to His Spirit that will determine the faithfulness of our walk, in the end.

If you are pursuing, seeking and fulfilling the purposes the Lord has ordained for you, He will be with you just as surely as He was with Joshua and David, and His Son Yeshua, who ran His race and completed **every** destiny assignment for which the Father sent Him to this broken world.

*Therefore, when He came into the world, He said: "Sacrifice and offering You did not desire, but **a body You have prepared for Me**. In* *burnt offerings and sacrifices for sin You had no pleasure. Then I said,* ***'Behold, I have come – In the volume of the book it is written of Me – to do Your will, O God.***'"(Heb.10:5-7).

I have glorified You on the earth. ***I have finished the work which You have given Me to do*** (Jn.17:4).

May we all be able to say these words at the end of our lives: "I have finished the work that You gave me to do, My Father." How blessed we will be if we can say those words. Amen.

Chapter 7
Discovering our Destiny

Then I said, "Behold, I come;
In the scroll of the book it is written of me.
Psalm 40:7 & Hebrews 10:7

Why Am I Here?

In our previous chapters, we have emphasized that one crucial factor in conquering fear is **knowing why you were born** for such a time as this. **It is a matter of destiny**, and of discovering that the Lord chose you and loved you before the worlds were formed. Not only did He create you, but He created you with a **Divine Purpose** in His heart.

Now, we will explore how we might know what the Lord has predestined for us, according to His purposes. If we never discover what those purposes are, we will be bored and unfulfilled. Additionally, and more troubling than boredom, is that when the time comes for us to give an account of our years on earth, we will have unbearable regret, for what we were meant to be, but never found out.

We must make sure this never happens. In discovering our destiny, we will overcome fear, because the Lord will help us in our struggles, fight for us when we encounter attack or opposition, and will go with us when we feel afraid to step out.

> ....*He* **chose us in Him before the foundation of the world**, *that we should be holy and without blame before Him in love, having* **predestined us to adoption as sons** *by Jesus Christ to Himself, according to the good pleasure* **of His will** *...In Him also we have* **obtained an inheritance**, *being* **predestined** *according to the* **purpose of Him** *who works* **all things according to the counsel of His will** (Eph.1:4-5,11).

The Lord chose us before the foundation of the world to be holy and blameless before Him. He also predestined us to become His adopted sons and daughters, through Yeshua, for this was His good and pleasing will.

The Lord also **ordained** for each of us **a unique purpose**, which was meant only for us to fulfill. Each individual was given his or her unique purpose and destiny before Creation. The Lord also prepared for us an imperishable inheritance, according to the counsel of His perfect will.

In one sense, knowing the purpose for which God made us is even more important than overcoming fear. But in discovering His purpose for our lives, we will begin to overcome all our fears without even trying.

It is so sad that a majority of believers go through their lives without ever asking the Lord, "What divine destiny was in Your heart when you chose me, before the foundation of the world?"

Another more poetic way of asking this question is: "What dream did You dream for me, my Father, before I was conceived?" But this is not poetry – it is reality, and we must know the answer. I sing about this theme in many of my songs, as you may have heard. *"Your heart dreamed a dream for me."*

A small number of people have known their destiny from childhood, by the prophetic Word of the Lord. Jeremiah was one of those individuals.

*Then the word of the Lord came to me, saying: "Before I formed you in the womb **I knew you;** before you were born **I sanctified you; I ordained you a prophet to the nations**"* (Jer. 1:4-5).

But most of us never received direct prophetic revelation in our youth. Therefore, we need to ask Him. Why didn't we ever ask this question? Because we didn't know we were **supposed** to ask this question. But according to Ephesians, we MUST ask this question!

Paul also wrote this same revelation to the Romans and also to his beloved son in the faith, Timothy.

*For whom He **foreknew**, He also **predestined** to be conformed to the image of His Son, that He might be the firstborn among many brethren. Moreover whom He predestined, these He also **called**; whom He called, these He also **justified**; and whom He justified, these He also **glorified**.* (Rom.8:29-30).

The Greek word "foreknew" is *"proginosko,"* (G4267) and Strong's Concordance defines it as: "to know beforehand, i.e. foresee; foreknow (ordain), know (before).

The Greek word "predestined" is *"proorizo,"* (G4309) and Strong's Concordance defines it as: predestinate, determine before, ordain.

Paul is telling us that the Lord **knew us** (before), **predestined or ordained** us (before), **called us** (beckoned us to receive Him and follow Him), **justified us** (made us righteous, though we were filthy), and **glorified us** (made us to shine in His glorious likeness, as we were created to be.) All this He predetermined in His noble heart before Creation! **He already knew us!** Such knowledge is too high and wonderful to comprehend, as King David also wrote.

...My frame was not hidden from You, when I was made in secret, and skillfully wrought in the lowest parts of the earth. ***Your eyes saw my substance, being yet unformed.*** *And* ***in Your book they all were written, the days fashioned for me, when as yet*** <u>***there were none of them***</u> (Ps.139:15-16).
You have hedged me, behind and before, and laid Your hand upon me. ***Such knowledge is too wonderful for me; it is high, I cannot attain it*** (vs.5-6).

Paul also wrote to Timothy, encouraging him to understand his holy calling, according to the purpose and grace given to him **before time began**.

Therefore do not be ashamed of the testimony of our Lord, nor of me His prisoner, but share with me in the sufferings for the gospel according to the power of God, who has ***saved us*** *and* ***called us*** *with a holy calling, not according to our works, but according to His own* ***purpose*** *and* ***grace*** <u>***which was given to us in Christ Jesus before time began***</u> (2Tim.1:8-9).

This passage clearly states that **we were given both purpose and grace before time began.** How can that be, since we wouldn't be born for thousands of years? This question is not something we can grasp or explain, and it is too high for us to attain. Nevertheless, it is the truth, according to the Word of God, and we simply need to believe it and walk in it. It will change the way we live our lives!
Now we have the full Scriptural understanding that we are not here as a matter of chance or the random choices of human parents.

But as many as received Him, to them He gave the right to become children of God, to those who believe in His name: who were born, not of blood, ***nor of the will of the flesh, nor of the will of man, but of God*** (Jn.1:12-13).

We were born for this time, and we must not waste a moment more. We cannot continue to live for ourselves or to grope through life without any clear sense of purpose.

I am also one who learned these things late in life, but thankfully, not too late to find His purposes for me and to begin to walk in them. We are never too old to turn from our self-centered ways and begin to live **wholly** for the Lord's good pleasure and purposes.

God Has Planted a Seed of Destiny

I spent almost 30 years as a believer, and I don't remember asking the Lord, "What is the destiny purpose I was born for?"

This was partly because I didn't realize I needed to ask. I was dull of heart, and although I wanted a purpose in life, I didn't know to seek the Lord. Additionally, I couldn't understand some of Paul's writings. His profound and lengthy sentences were too complicated for me. I never prayed to receive the wisdom needed to understand what Paul was telling us. Now, later in life, I have grown to understand them from awesome teachers, who have taught much about fulfilling our destinies.

During my early years as a believer, there were no teachers or pastors in my life who taught on this matter of destiny. There were no internet teachings as we have now. I read excellent books, but I don't remember learning these matters of destiny. There is awesome teaching available on this subject now, Praise God.

If I had understood sooner, I wouldn't have trudged through so many years of my believing life, living in dullness, depression, and in some degree of compromise.

However, the Lord had **planted destiny seeds in me at a young age, years before I would be saved**. During those early years, I sensed that I was meant to help people or to do something "good."

I even had an idea that I was to serve God because my father had told me that God existed. In my childhood, I had tried to communicate with God in my bed at night, ever since I knew He existed. I couldn't hear His voice, and I didn't know what the Lord had ordained for me. **But the seed of destiny was there**. I believe this is true for all of us, whether we recognized it or not. I also wanted to sing and write my own songs, which was also a seed of destiny, and He has caused it to blossom in these latter years.

After receiving the Lord, I finished college, then graduate school, got married, and worked as a technical instructor in a corporation. I believe this job was the "teacher seed" that the Lord had ordained for me. He knew I would become a teacher of His Word. My Master's Degree was in Education, and the Lord was preparing me to become one of His teachers in the future. During my early married years, I was involved in attending believing prayer meetings or a congregation, and I tried to nourish my spirit.

After five years in the corporate world, the Lord called us to move to Israel. This testimony is shared in my first book, "Coffee Talks with Messiah." While living in Israel, I gave birth to my three children, and worked small part-time jobs at home while raising the babies. Most of my work was teaching piano, guitar, and teaching English to Israeli youths after school. Ten years earlier, when I had been a teenager in America, I also had taught guitar lessons at summer camp. The seed of teaching, playing, and singing music was starting to form, even before my salvation.

When our family later returned to America, I once again began teaching music lessons, as well as teaching other subjects in several schools. At one point, I returned to being a technical instructor in a different company, but it was too time-consuming for me to keep up with my responsibilities at home with three almost-teenagers. So I went back to teaching in schools, where the hours matched my children's schedules.

It turns out that teaching music, writing songs, and singing/producing worship music, as well as teaching the Word of God and writing books, has become the center of my destiny assignments now. These works were directly commissioned by the Lord. I even wrote a book in which I teach people how to write worship music: "The Priestly Songwriter."

My mother was trained to be a concert pianist, and she had given me music lessons since I was young. The Lord used these piano lessons profoundly in my future, although when I was young, I didn't put enough effort into practicing piano in the basement. But little did I know that it would become one of the greatest gifts of my life, and a beautiful tool to minister healing, love, and intimacy to the Lord's people, decades later. He uses **all things** for our good!

I believe each of you can recognize the special seeds the Lord planted in your heart in your early years. If you cannot yet find them, begin to ask your Beloved, "Lord, what works did you purpose for me to do for Your Kingdom, for Your people? What seeds and natural gifts did you give me that would prepare me for this destiny, which You have reserved just for me?"

I Have Come to Do Your Will, O God

David had deep revelation of our eternal purposes in God. Psalm 40 speaks about the destiny of the coming Messiah, the Lord Yeshua. But it also speaks about us. We are predestined to walk in the same obedience and consecration in which the Lord Yeshua walked during His days on earth (see Eph.1:4-5). The words of this psalm were true for David, they are true for Lord Yeshua, and I am convinced they are also true for us.

Sacrifice and offering You did not desire; my ears You have opened. [our spiritual ears must be open to hear His voice; to hear and obey is better than sacrifice.] *Burnt offering and sin offering You did not require.*
Then I said, "Behold, I come; **in the scroll of the book** it is *written of me. I delight to do Your will, O my God, and Your law* is *within my heart."* (Ps.40:6-8).

It is written in the scroll of Messiah's life what He would accomplish on earth. But it is also written in each of **our** heavenly scrolls of destiny what we were meant to accomplish on earth. Though it is written in Heaven, this doesn't guarantee that we will automatically **know** or **fulfill** all we were meant to do. We have free will, and the Lord will never force us to pursue and accomplish all that He originally dreamed for us. That is why we must seek Him and pray, just as the Lord Yeshua prayed often to His Father, to know and to do His good pleasure. As He *was* in the world, so must we be.

He who says he abides in Him ought himself also to walk just as He walked (1Jn.2:6).

If we are walking in His will, we will be given the grace to overcome the natural fears that come at us. In Chapter 3, we saw that the great heroes of faith – Abraham, Moses, Joshua, David, Paul, and others – were commanded not to fear. The Lord assured them He had gone ahead of them, was fighting for them, and had ordained the victory.

In other cases, such as Esther and Gideon, they were afraid, but they overcame the fear and did it anyway. That is true courage, by the way. But through Bible history and beyond, **the way His people overcome fear is by knowing He is with them and that He will never forsake them.**

This is just as true for the martyrs as it is for those who emerge triumphant from the threat of battle. The overcomers know they are walking in the Lord's calling in their life; they are doing what He purposed for them in His heart. **They know they are walking in their destiny.** Knowing this makes all the difference. That is how they overcome fear, by this confidence and by His grace.

I Don't Know if I Am on the Lord's Chosen Path

You might wonder, "But what if the Lord has not sent me to do a specific Kingdom task? What if I'm living my normal life and not going out into battle like ancient Israel? How can I know He will go ahead of me? How can I be sure He will fight my battles? How can I not be afraid?"

This is a very understandable question that many of us could ask. We have several thoughtful answers to consider.

The first step would be to take a wider view of the **purposes that motivate your life and your planning for the future.** Be honest with yourself, as you consider your motivations for your plans and activities. Just this first step will help you see your life more clearly through the Lord's eyes, especially if you pray to Him before you make this assessment.

Set some quality time aside, sit or kneel before the Lord, and let Him review your life with you. This will be very fruitful and will help you to quickly evaluate your priorities in life. Talk to Him as you would talk to your best friend – because HE IS!

Write in a journal anything the Holy Spirit brings to your mind – perhaps an area or activity in your life that He shows you is not in His will. Keep notes on all the things He will show you. Remember, **it delights the Lord that you are seeking His heart** and wanting to know how He evaluates your life, your motivations, your activities, and your attitudes.

Wouldn't you want to find out NOW if there is some aspect of your life that is not in obedience with His perfect will? Would you want to wait till you meet the Lord to find out? Of course not!

Although we live each day in a fairly predictable way, is there a larger purpose in the Kingdom of God for our lives? Are we doing what the Lord has expressly directed us to do? Are we just trying to survive, financially or otherwise? Have we ever asked the Lord for our Kingdom assignments?

Just as I shared about the early destiny seeds the Lord planted in my life, think about the activities and themes that stir you, that motivate you. Things you feel deeply in your inner spirit – a sense of calling or destiny – something you were meant to do. These are strong clues about God's heavenly, pre-ordained assignments for you. What do you love? What is your passion? Depending on how you answer these questions, you might discover what the Lord has already planted in your heart. Of course, if you love something unclean, that is a temptation from the enemy or your own flesh, but it is not a destiny seed of God. But as long as it's something wholesome or neutral, the Lord may be giving you whispers of His Plan as you quiet yourself before Him.

God's Perfect Will?

I believe there are two levels of being "in God's will." We can be in His *perfect will*, or we can be in His *"permissive will."* The permissive will is what the Lord lets His people do, without negative consequences, at least for some time. He is not the author of these choices, but He has given man free will.

"Permissive" implies that these choices are not inherently sinful, and He does not forbid them. Sinful choices include fornication, cursing, lying, addictions, pornography, cheating, or stealing. If a believer is engaged in these types of inherently sinful behaviors, it is never His permissive will. This term applies to more neutral things, like babysitting the grandchildren, playing on a sports team or coaching a team, joining a book club where secular books are read, visiting historical sites in your nation, watching your favorite drama on TV every week, never missing an episode. You can think of many other "neutral" activities. However, not all TV shows are "neutral." There are many things the Lord does not want us to watch, even if they are not fully evil.

For example, I used to be "addicted" to a weekly show in the U.S. called "24." It was a brilliant thriller about a high-level government agent trying to stop deadly acts of global terror, nuclear or bio-destruction of masses of people, or assassinations. Each one-hour episode gave us one literal hour in the "real-time" schedule of this hero's activities, in trying to stop this terror event.

On the next week's show, we would see the next hour in his day, and a week later, the third hour of his day, and so on, for 24 weeks of shows. It was an awesome show, and I couldn't wait for it to come on each week. No one in the show ever had time to sleep, due to the terror threat, so the whole 24 hours were filled with activity, not sleep. The actors wore the same clothes in every episode, because it all took place on one day of their lives, hour by hour.

The problem was, I would lie awake at night, thinking about the events, the dangers, the characters, and I didn't want to ever miss one episode. **The Lord convicted me to stop watching it altogether.** He told me it was robbing me of all my concentration on Him and on "real life." I was too obsessed with the thrilling storyline and its characters. I stopped completely, and never watched it again.

I'm telling you this because I loved that show, and it was the highlight of my week, but the Lord was jealous for my mind and heart. Also, this show was about violent terrorists and heinous plans to murder millions of people. The Lord didn't want me "spending time" with terrorists, even if they got caught in the end.

If I had disobeyed the Lord and continued to watch it, my life would not have turned out the way it is now, because my heart would have rejected the Word of the Lord for **my** life. Maybe other believers could get away with watching it, but I was not permitted to watch it, no matter what others might do. This is about obedience, and He is serious about it.

Movies are a topic similar to the TV testimony shared above. I will leave that topic to your conscience. But remember that God's holy eyes cannot look upon evil. Don't think He will come to the movies with you if your eyes enjoy watching evil deeds, even if the bad guys get caught later. If the movie or TV show has sexual scenes or spoken parts that curse or take the Lord's Name in vain, I know from personal experience that the Lord expects me to turn it off **immediately**. He won't watch it, He won't listen to it, and He won't be near to us.

These activities would not be the Lord's perfect will for how we spend our time. I'm only using these as examples, not as judgments against these neutral activities.

In cases where the believer is in a sinful lifestyle or not walking with the Lord at all, he or she is completely *out of His will*. This would be a terribly dangerous condition to live in. Ananias and Sapphira were out of God's will and in presumptuous sin when they lied to Peter (and to the Holy Spirit) about the amount of money they sold their property for. They were both struck dead on that same day. This is the most dangerous situation for a professing believer.

Here are some examples of being in God's will, from Scripture, which will help us examine our own lives. The assessments I share below are my own opinions, regarding whether each biblical figure was in God's perfect will or His permissive will. My opinion on these cases is not necessarily how the Lord views them, but these are my best conclusions, based on the information the Bible provides.

A. Moses walked completely in the perfect will of the Lord. The only exception was when he struck the rock 40 years later when he had been commanded to speak to the rock. The Lord still brought forth water from the rock for the congregation, even though Moses disobeyed Him. I would not say that this act was God's "permissive will." Moses was out of the will of God at that moment. The Lord once showed me that He felt dishonored when Moses disobeyed Him and struck the rock in his anger. The Lord didn't have to reward that disobedience; He didn't have to give them water. But He couldn't bear to let His people die of thirst, and so He gave them the water anyway. However, Moses was tragically punished for this and was not permitted to enter the Promised Land.

B. As far as we know, Joshua was in the perfect will of God for his entire period of leadership and wars, as they conquered the Promised Land. Therefore, the Lord was with him in every battle. Their only failure in one battle was due to the sin of one man.

In Joshua 6 and 7, the Lord commanded the Israelites not to touch the plunder after Jericho was destroyed (Jos. 6:18). One Israelite man, Achan, secretly took some of the spoil and hid it in his tent. No one knew and when the army tried to take the next city, they were driven back and some were killed, due to the sin in the camp. Joshua prayed, and Achan's sin was revealed; he and his household were stoned to death. This one man's sin cost the lives of 36 innocent Israelite soldiers. After that purging, Israel won every battle and war.

C. King David was out of the will of God and was in sin when he committed adultery with Bathsheba. The consequences were disastrous and punishing.

D. King David was in the perfect will of God to prepare everything for the building of the Temple, and not to attempt to build it himself. He obeyed God, though he had wanted to build it.

E. King Solomon was in the perfect will of God when he built the Temple in exact alignment with the plans his father David had received from the Spirit of the Lord.

F. King Solomon was out of the will of God when he married hundreds of foreign wives and took concubines. The Lord did not approve of this, but He allowed Solomon to do this. Even so, the Lord knew that this choice would lead to outright sin and being out of the will of God. Since the Lord had commanded His people not to marry the daughters of the Canaanites, Solomon was in direct disobedience to the Word of God. (It was not a sin to marry the daughter of Egypt, but it was a sin to marry Canaanite women.) It is likely that Solomon was completely out of the will of God in doing this, though the Lord permitted it and didn't punish him during his lifetime.

As King, he should have set a higher example to the people. Because of his position, the Lord gave tremendous grace to Solomon and allowed him much freedom, but I believe he was out of God's will in these foreign marriages.

G. The follow-up to these marriages was that King Solomon was completely out of the will of God when he was seduced into idolatry by these foreign wives. Solomon was rebuked by the Lord at the end of his reign. It was only God's mercy and promise to David, that He allowed Solomon to complete his 40-year reign. After his death, Israel was torn apart and remained in civil war for many years. The wisest man in the world, whom the Lord visited personally twice in his life, went after the gods of the Canaanite wives he married. Where did his wisdom go? He even saw the Lord, as few have, yet he sinned. He started well, but King Solomon did NOT finish his race well. This is a warning to us all.

H. King Jehoshaphat was a righteous king of Judah, and Scripture honors him as having done "what was right in the eyes of the Lord." There were many times he acted in the perfect will of the Lord. However, there were three recorded incidents in Jehoshaphat's life that were clearly not the "perfect will" of God and were dangerous and damaging in some cases. The Lord permitted him to make three wrongful alliances with Ahab's dynasty, but we must discover if he was out of the will of God, or if he was operating under His "permissive will."

> 1. He allied himself in marriage to the daughter of Ahab, the wicked king of Israel. She was named Athaliah and much later, she became a murderous queen mother, almost destroying the entire line of Judaic kings. The Lord did not seem to punish or rebuke him for this marriage so that it may have been in His "permissive will." However, the Lord knew all the brutal murders of the royal family that Athaliah would commit later in her life.
>
> 2. He allied himself again with Ahab (his father-in-law,) by agreeing to go to war with him against Ramot Gilead (see 2Chr.18:1-34). The results were disastrous and fatal for Ahab, but the Lord delivered Jehoshaphat alive from the battle. However, the prophet of God rebuked Jehoshaphat for this

alliance, after the fact. Since he was rebuked by the prophet, he was out of God's will.

3. Near the end of his life, he allied himself with another wicked king of Israel, named Ahaziah. They built trading ships together as a joint business venture. Another prophet rebuked him for this, and although the Lord allowed him to build the ships, the Lord wrecked the ships, and they never sailed (see 2Chr. 20:35-37). Since the prophet rebuked him, he was out of the will of God, and the Lord destroyed his work.

Finding His Perfect Will

In these biblical cases, apart from Moses and Joshua, there was mixture in most of their lives, but David was by far the most exemplary. In some ways, these leaders were not so different from us, in the complex situations that caused them either to sin or simply stray from the Lord's best purposes. We also saw how severe their problems became when they were out of the Lord's perfect will.

You might not see how the lives of these ancient Israelite judges and kings connect to our lives. However, the principles of loving and serving the Lord have never changed. The principles of needing to know the will of God and then, to obediently follow it, have never changed.

Time is actually one of our greatest gifts. Each of us is allotted a certain amount of time on this earth and usually, we do not know how long that will be. Therefore, it would be tragic to waste large sections of our life, always thinking we have more time ahead to get into God's perfect will. That time might never come. Scripture tells us so many times, this one warning:

Therefore, as the Holy Spirit says: "**Today,** *if you will hear His voice,* ***do not harden your hearts*** *as in the rebellion, in the day of trial in the wilderness, where your fathers tested Me, tried Me, and saw My works forty years* (Heb.3:7-9).

If someone is walking a path **outside of the will of the Lord** for their life – if they are walking a path the Lord never intended for them to walk – how can they feel confident that He will fight for them? Our Lord is very merciful, even in less than ideal situations. But His protection is not automatic, though it is available for all who call on His Name.

The Lord is the Same: Yesterday, Today and Forever

The Lord is exactly the same Person in both the Old and New Testaments. He doesn't have two different personalities or two different standards for His people's obedience. He is the same, yesterday, today and forever.

There are many Christians who make an artificial dichotomy between the moral standards of the God of the Old Testament and the moral standards of the Lord Yeshua in the New Testament. This is a heresy, and it endangers all believers who fall into this false doctrine. To avoid confusion, when I say "moral standards," I'm not referring to certain ceremonial laws in the Old Testament that are not required of us, nor are they even possible in our society. I'm speaking of matters of the heart: sexual purity, integrity, honesty, genuine love and caring, generosity, tithing to God, humility, and other such heart matters. In these matters, His standards are the same.

Hebrews tells us that the Lord Yeshua is the same, yesterday, today and forever. He and His Father are ONE. They have the same thought, the same character, and the same standards for obedience, holiness, and honesty. Do not listen to any teachers who say that the Old Testament is not relevant to our lives today, or that tithing was only for the Old Testament.

***All Scripture is given by inspiration of God, and is profitable for doctrine, for reproof, for correction, for instruction** in righteousness, that the man of God may be **complete**, thoroughly equipped for every good work* (2Tim.3:16-17).

When Paul wrote these words ("*All Scripture...*") to Timothy, the only written Scripture that existed at that time was the Old Testament. We need to know the **whole Counsel of God**, to have a balanced walk and theology, regarding God's standards.

Let's close our discussion with this: It is **never acceptable** to be deliberately out of God's perfect will. If we **know** His will for us, and yet we don't do it, the Lord Yeshua said we would be punished severely. If we **don't know**, it is our responsibility to ask Him until we do know. This might take some time, or He may reveal it to you swiftly, but He's worth waiting for.

*And that servant who **knew** **his** **master's** **will**, and did not prepare himself or do according to his will, shall be beaten with many stripes. But he who **did not know**, yet committed things deserving* *of stripes, shall be beaten with few. For everyone to whom much is given, from him much will be required* (Lk.12:47-48).

We must take this warning seriously. Most of you who would read this book are likely serious about pleasing the Lord and making sure you are in His perfect will, as much as possible. I need this warning as much as anyone.

Let us intentionally check our hearts with the Lord. Who are we living for? For ourselves or for the Lord, who created us with a purpose and destiny in His heart? If we are living for ourselves, how can we presume that His blessing, provision, and protection will remain upon us?

Each of us must go to the Lord with these hard questions:

What have You sent me to do?

What have You ordained for me to do, and how can I step into it?

What are my heavenly assignments, and why am I on this earth for such a time as this?

Isn't the Lord still with us in all the ups and downs of our lives, even when we gradually drift away from intimacy, without meaning to? Yes. He is always with us, He always loves us, and His mercies are new every morning. **But His blessings and protection are not automatic**. Psalm 34 tells us that "the Angel of the Lord encamps around those who fear Him." To fear the Lord is to honor and obey His choices in our lives. When we are intentionally walking in His perfect will, to the best of our discernment, He will send angelic help to guard us in all our ways. Casual and careless believers cannot be compared to the fighting men of Israel, who went out to war with the Lord's explicit command and with it, His promise of protection, blessing, and victory. We cannot presume that He will respond to all our activities and desires in the same way – it all depends on **what has He called us to do, and on our responses to Him.** Amen.

Chapter 8
The Fear of the Lord

The angel of the Lord encamps all around those who fear Him
And He delivers them.
Psalm 34:7

This chapter will be a key to **overcoming fear** by helping us to understand how to walk in the **"Fear of the Lord."** There is a world of difference between our normal fears in life and the Fear of the Lord. We began to discuss this in Chapter 3, but we'll dig deeper now.

The concept of "walking in the Fear of the Lord" is found often in Scripture, appearing well over 100 times. For example:

*The **fear of the Lord is the beginning of wisdom**, and **the knowledge of the Holy One is understanding** (Prov 9:10).*

This proverb shows us that **fearing** the Lord and **knowing** Him are one and the same. This means we will never attain wisdom and understanding if we do not fear the Lord and intimately know Him. No one who claims to be wise, but does not fear the Lord, is truly wise. Even the most brilliant scientist has no real wisdom, apart from the fear of the Lord. They may have intelligence, but they do not have wisdom, as God defines wisdom.

Let's first look at one special case of the Fear of the Lord.

"The Fear of Isaac"

In two references to the lives of the Patriarchs, the Lord is called "the Fear of Isaac." Normally, He is known as "the God of Abraham, Isaac, and Jacob." But Jacob calls God by this Name: The FEAR of his father, Isaac. We see this only once in history, but there is a profound message for each of us.

In Genesis 22, we read the account of Abraham's greatest test: Would he obey the Lord's word and sacrifice his son, Isaac, although he was the promised son, through whom all Abraham's descendants were to come?

As the two of them went on together, Isaac spoke up and said to his father, Abraham, "Father?"

"Yes, my son," Abraham replied.

"The fire and the wood are here," Isaac said, "but where is the lamb for the burnt offering?"

Abraham answered, "God himself will provide the lamb, for the burnt offering, my son." And the two of them went on together. When they reached the place God had told him about, Abraham built an altar there and arranged the wood on it. He bound his son, Isaac and laid him on the altar on top of the wood. Then he reached out his hand and took the knife to slay his son (Gen.22: 6b-10, NIV).

We know the angel of the Lord stopped Abraham at the last second. This was as close as he could have come to slaying his own son. It is evident that the fear of this event stayed with Isaac for the rest of his life.

Isaac's son Jacob worked 20 years for his unscrupulous uncle, Laban. Jacob had been cheated out of his wife, his wages, and had been living in conditions of deprivation. After fleeing from Laban and getting caught, the two men made a covenant. Notice the **three** different Names, by which Jacob refers to God, in this argument:

*"If the **God of my father**, the **God of Abraham** and the **Fear of Isaac** had not been with me, you would surely have sent me away empty handed"* (Gen.31:42a, NIV).

This is interesting because *"the God of my father"* also refers to Isaac's God, but Jacob adds, *"and the Fear of Isaac."*

Soon after, when Laban and Jacob took an oath together, we read that *"Jacob swore by **the Fear of his father Isaac*** (Gen.31:53, NIV).

Nowhere else in Scripture is the Lord given this title. Since Jacob was Isaac's son, it is likely he grew up hearing his father referring to the Lord as, "my Fear," or saying to his sons, "The Lord is my Fear." Jacob had a reason for referring to the Lord this way, using a different title for Abraham's God than for Isaac's God. Of course, there is only one God, but He goes by many Names, depending on what attribute of God is being emphasized. Jacob knew his father Isaac had walked in the Fear of the Lord, more than any man.

Once, I was listening to a teaching about the Fear of the Lord, and I received a revelation from the Lord. He showed me Isaac and began to teach me why Jacob used this expression. Isaac's fear stayed with him his entire life, since the day his father lifted up the knife to slay him. He was a moment away from slaughter, at the hands of the one he loved. He had been bound, laid on a pile of wood, and about to become a burnt offering.

Isaac had previously seen his father lay sheep on the altar, on occasions of worship or consecration. He had seen his father cut their throats, spill their blood, and set fire to the wood. He had watched the entire sheep disappear in the flames. This was a traumatic experience.

We would never judge Abraham for this act, for he was simply obeying God. But Isaac would never be the same. He feared the God of Abraham more than we can grasp.

In God's mercy, a ram suddenly appeared in the thickets to save his life. Abraham had previously told his son, while still walking toward the mountain, *"God will provide the lamb."*

Isaac was redeemed by a ram. If God had rescued you from death at the last second, you would walk in the Fear of the Lord always.

But we are also rescued ones. We were under the death sentence of condemnation and eternal torment. God provided a Lamb to die in our place, to save our lives. The Lamb was Yeshua. Do we understand what the Lord did for us, and do we walk continually in the Fear of the Lord, as Isaac did? I believe the Lord would want us all to walk in this awareness. We were rescued from death, just as surely as Isaac was.

The Fear of the Lord

The Bible used this term frequently when referring to people who found favor with the Lord. It usually refers to Israelites, but we also find that non-Jews, both men and women of various ranks in society, also feared the God of Israel. The Egyptian midwives feared the Lord. Job feared the Lord, as did the Roman centurion, Cornelius. There are at least 58 references to the Fear of the Lord in the Psalms alone, and countless more elsewhere. Here are just a few of these.

And now, Israel, **what does the Lord your God require of you, but to fear the Lord your God,** *to walk in all His ways and to* **love Him***, to serve the Lord your God with* **all your heart** *and with all your soul* (Deut.10:12).

You can see that the Lord **requires** us to fear Him – it is His fundamental requirement, from which springs walking in His ways, loving Him and serving Him. It is not optional.

*Behold, the **eye of the Lord is on those who fear Him**, on those who hope in His mercy. The angel of the Lord **encamps all around those who fear Him**, and He delivers them.* (Ps.33:18, 34:7).

His eye is upon us if we fear the Lord and hope in His mercy. Fearing the Lord gives us confidence that we **will** obtain mercy. We believe He is good, and we fear Him with love. If we fear the Lord, we will have His angel close to us, assigned to keep us safe and deliver us.

"Many daughters have done well, but you excel them all." Charm is deceitful and beauty is passing, **but a woman who fears the Lord, she shall be praised**. *Give her of the fruit of her hands, and let her own works praise her in the gates* (Prov.31:29-31).

The beautiful heart of a God-fearing woman of any age is precious to the Lord. Believing girls and women must carefully guard their motives and always walk in the Fear of the Lord. They should never use beauty or charm to manipulate men. Additionally, a man who fears the Lord cannot be manipulated by charm or beauty, so it works both ways.

Then the king of Egypt spoke to the Hebrew midwives, of whom the name of one was Shiphrah and the name of the other Puah; and he said, "When you do the duties of a midwife for the Hebrew women, and see them on the birthstools, if it is a son, then you shall kill him; but if it is a daughter, then she shall live." **But the midwives feared God,** *and did not do as the king of Egypt commanded them, but saved the male children alive...Therefore,* **God dealt well with the midwives,** *and the people multiplied and grew very mighty. And so it was,* **because the midwives feared God,** *that He provided households for them* (Ex.1:15-17, 20-21).

The Lord is no respecter of people, regarding race, nationality, or gender. These Egyptian midwives were under Pharaoh's orders to kill every male Hebrew baby. They could have been imprisoned for disobeying a direct order he spoke to them. They feared the God of the Hebrews, who was the One True God. They didn't fear the gods of the Egyptians, nor even the power of Pharaoh himself. They had the Fear of the Lord, and wouldn't harm these babies. Look how the Lord honored and rewarded them. He even told us their names, so that when we read this story, we will always remember Shiphrah and Puah.

*Then Saul said to Samuel, "I have sinned, for I have transgressed the commandment of the Lord and your words, because **I feared the people and obeyed their voice**** (1Sam.15:24).

This statement is tremendously significant. Saul didn't fear the commandment of the Lord. Rather, he feared the people, and because **he feared them, he obeyed their voice**. The Fear of Man is a snare to us. The Fear of the Lord is our only safety.

*Oh, that they had such a heart in them **that they would fear Me** and always keep all My commandments, that it might be well with them and with their children forever!* (Deut.5:29).

Can you hear the ache in the Lord's heart? He deeply yearns for them to fear Him so that it would go well for them and their children forever. If they do not fear Him, it will not go well for them and their children. Can we see that it is to our great benefit to genuinely fear the Lord?

***The fear of the Lord is to hate evil**; pride and arrogance and the evil way and the perverse mouth I hate. **The fear of the Lord prolongs days**, but the years of the wicked will be shortened* (Prov.8:13, 10:27).

If we fear the Lord, we will hate what is evil, which includes pride, arrogance, and perverse speech. And our lives will be lengthened.

*But the other, answering, rebuked him, saying, "**Do you not even fear God**, seeing you are under the same condemnation?* (Lk.23:40).

The humble thief on the cross rebuked the reproachful thief by saying, *"Don't you **fear God?**"* The humble thief knew that after they expired on the cross, they would both have to answer to God's judgment. Their troubles would not be over after death, and the humble thief was justified that day before he died.

*"**Fear God** and give Him glory, because **the hour of His judgments has come**."*

The angels in the book of Revelation warn the last-days inhabitants of the earth to **fear God**. Even in the hour of His judgments, some hardened hearts will still not fear God. This is why the angels are giving mankind one last opportunity to **fear the Lord**. If we walk in the fear of the Lord, He will comfort us, and we will be multiplied.

Then the churches throughout all Judea, Galilee, and Samaria had peace and were edified. ***And walking in the fear of the Lord** and in the **comfort of the Holy Spirit, they were multiplied*** (Acts 9:31).
***The fear of the Lord is clean**, enduring forever; the judgments of the Lord are true and righteous altogether* (Ps.19:9).

The fear of the Lord is clean – it is a pure, healthy fear, completely different from demonic, tormenting fear. "Clean" also means that it brings no condemnation, but it brings a desire to repent and stay close to the Lord's heart. It goes together with loving Him and being loved by Him.

Should We Fear Punishment?

The answer to this question is: "Yes and no." The explanation is complex, but it will make sense. In Luke 12:4-5, the Lord Yeshua gives us His perspective on physical death versus eternal death in hell – eternal punishment.

*"And I say to you, My friends, **do not be afraid of those who kill the body**, and after that have no more that they can do. But I will show you whom you should fear: **Fear Him** who, after He has killed, **has power to cast into hell**; yes, I say to you, **fear Him**!* (Lk.12:4-5).

Matthew adds two more details to this teaching:
*"And do not fear those who kill the body but **cannot kill the soul**. But rather **fear Him** who is **able to destroy both soul and body in hell*** (Mt.10:28).

The Lord is teaching that we must **overcome our fear of physical death** on this earth, even if wicked people murder us. He needs us to understand that once a person dies, no one on earth can ever hurt him again. But once our soul leaves our body, God now has the power to destroy both body and soul in Hell, which is a punishment that never ends.

Yeshua is comparing the fear of temporary earthly suffering and death, to eternal suffering, from which we never escape or recover. That is why He gives this difficult teaching. He is actually saying: *"**The way to overcome your fear of what people can do to you, is to fear the Lord, who has the power to save or destroy your soul, which continues after your death, forevermore.**"*

You might remember what I shared in Chapter 3: That we should fear the Lord in a loving, reverential way, not wanting to hurt Him or dishonor Him. I explained that the Lord doesn't want us to obey Him only because we fear punishment. Now, as we look at the Lord's word above, it might seem like a contradiction. Yeshua is telling us to fear God, who can punish us eternally. We spoke briefly about this seeming paradox in Chapter 3, but let's go a little deeper, and we will understand how both can be true.

Punishment is Never God's Goal

In a healthy Parent-Child relationship, the parent wants the child to obey out of love, respect, and obedience. A loving parent doesn't want their children to obey, merely because they fear punishment. The good parent wants them to obey because they respect their parents and don't want to dishonor them. Most children, sadly, only fear punishment, as I feared my father's spanking when I was very little. I didn't care if my bad behavior grieved him; I only feared punishment.

However, my fear of punishment kept me from acting badly again. I don't remember ever getting another spanking after that. The point is that fearing punishment can be helpful in improving our behavior, but it doesn't really change our heart from wicked to good. It only changes our behavior.

The Lord knows all our thoughts, as well as our behavior. If we want to be found faithful in the Lord's eyes, it isn't enough to merely stop behaving badly. We must examine our motives and the thoughts of our heart, which the Lord hears loud and clear. This is a deeper level of fearing the Lord when we repent and realign our thoughts, as well as our deeds.

Can a professing believer do good deeds and even do power works by the Holy Spirit, and still be cast out of His Presence on Judgment Day? The answer is "yes," for those who do not bear the inward fruit of righteousness and holiness in their private lives, despite their outward signs and power. This is why we must walk in the Fear of the Lord, knowing His eyes are always upon us, whether human eyes see us or not.

*"Not everyone who says to Me, 'Lord, Lord,' shall enter the kingdom of heaven, but **he who does the will of My Father in heaven**. Many will say to Me in that day, 'Lord, Lord, have we not prophesied in Your name, cast out demons in Your name, and done many wonders in Your name?' And then I will declare to them, **'I never knew you; depart from Me, you who practice lawlessness!'**"(Mt.7:21-23).*

The sincere Fear of the Lord, showing reverence and not wanting to hurt or disappoint our Father, is truly the BEST motive for obeying. It is a much nobler motivation than fearing punishment. The Lord is well-pleased when we fear Him in this loving way.

Nevertheless, if a person is rebellious and living a lawless lifestyle, it is **far better** that they fear the eternal punishment of hell than not fearing God at all. It is impossible to exaggerate the levels of suffering in hell, and we are helping all people by warning them. The Lord Yeshua spoke more about hell, condemnation, and the Lake of Fire than all the Old Testament prophets, although they spoke quite a bit about it, too.

In the passage below, the Lord Yeshua is partially quoting from the last words of the prophet Isaiah, concerning the unquenchable fire in hell, and the worms that never die.

*" If your hand causes you to sin, cut it off. It is better for you to enter into life maimed, rather than having two hands, **to go to hell, into the fire that shall never be quenched** – where 'Their worm does not die, and the fire is not quenched.'"* (Mk.9:43-44).

Why are many "Christian" teachers and prophets teaching that hell is not a real place, but just a "state of mind?" Or teaching that Satan will eventually be redeemed? Why are others teaching that hell is a temporary punishment, but that later, people are "cleansed by the fire," learn their lesson, and get to heaven eventually? It is popular to teach that eventually, everyone ends up in Heaven because a loving God could never put someone in hell permanently. The name of this doctrine is "Universal Reconciliation." It is false teaching.

Those who teach these falsehoods should know the word of God, and yet they teach this publicly. Are we helping people or hurting them with these false messages?

Our Lord Himself plainly confirmed that hell is a real place and that the torment is never-ending. How can these Christian leaders boldly teach these doctrines that are contradicted by the words of Yeshua Himself?

The Lord does not want His people to fear His punishment. No loving parent wants their children to fear punishment, and our God is a good Father. He wants them to love Him and fear Him, but from a heart of knowing His goodness and kindness, not His harshness and punishment. He doesn't want to frighten them into loving Him. Love must be voluntary, or it is not love. He will not force anyone, but He lovingly warns everyone that hell is a real place. He paid the most terrible price to keep anyone from having to go there, and if hell weren't real or eternal, the Lord would not have had to suffer such an agonizing death to buy us back from this fate.

The amazing conclusion is this: **The key to overcoming fear is to Fear the Lord.**

They Shall Be Mine

*Then **those who feared the LORD** spoke to one another, and the LORD listened and heard them; so **a book of remembrance was written** before Him **for those who fear the LORD** and who meditate on His name.*

*"They shall be Mine," says the LORD of hosts, "on the day that **I make them My jewels**. And **I will spare them** as a man spares his own son who serves him." Then you shall again discern between the righteous and the wicked, between one who serves God and one who does not serve Him* (Mal.3:16-18).

This is a remarkable passage. In Hebrew, the word for "jewels" is "*segulah*." Strong's Concordance defines this word (H5459) as: "peculiar treasure; special; jewel; particular treasure." This is the same word the Lord used about His people in Exodus 19 when He promised that they would be His royal priesthood, His set-apart, precious people:

*Now therefore, if you will indeed obey My voice and keep My covenant, then you shall be a **special treasure (segulah)** to Me above all people, for all the earth is Mine* (Ex.19:5).

In Malachi 3:16-18, we see that those who **feared the Lord** would be **spared** in the **day of trouble**, but those who did not fear Him would not be spared. The Lord will make a distinction between the righteous and the wicked, and those who fear the Lord will be counted as righteous. **Those who fear the Lord will obtain mercy.**

Lord Yeshua Had the Fear of the Lord

Isaiah prophesied that the coming Messiah would be filled with the seven Spirits of God. (see Isa.11:1-3). One of these Spirits is "The Fear of the Lord." Simply put, this means that the Lord Yeshua would walk in the Fear of the Lord for all of His days.

There shall come forth a Rod from the stem of Jesse, and a Branch shall grow out of his roots. The **Spirit of the Lord** *shall rest upon Him, the* **Spirit of wisdom** *and* **understanding***, the* **Spirit of counsel** *and* **might***, the* **Spirit of knowledge** *and of* <u>*the Fear of the Lord. His delight is in the fear of the Lord*</u> (Isa.11:1-3a).

Throughout the Lord Yeshua's ministry on earth, He was consumed with a **desire to obey His Father**, at all costs. The Lord said He had come only to do His Father's will. His words and deeds were not of His own initiative, for He did only what He saw and heard the Father doing. This is the outworking of the Fear of the Lord in all His words and deeds. Speaking of the Fear of the Lord during Yeshua's earthly life, the writer of Hebrews says:

In the days of His flesh, when He had offered up prayers and supplications, with vehement cries and tears to Him who was able to save Him from death, ***and was heard because of the Fear of God which was in Him.****"* (Heb.5:7, AP).

This passage gives us a painful and intimate glimpse of the inner prayer life and anguished emotions of the Lord Yeshua, as a real man, as a son of His Father in the human sense. He went to lonely places in the middle of the night ("a great while before dawn"), and He wept aloud and cried out to His Father for help and deliverance, in the reverent Fear of the Lord. He was an example for us, as to how we also should interact with our Father from our deepest emotions, offered in holiness and with reverent fear.

In our last chapter, we looked at some biblical warnings to keep us in the fear of the Lord. Let us look at a few more examples of the consequences of not fearing the Lord.

Isaiah Contrasts Two Opposite Versions of Fear

Isaiah 33 is a remarkable passage, likely referring to the times we live in now. It includes a warning of judgment on the sinful people in Israel, but it also gives a precious promise to those who fear Him. These words are as applicable for the Body of Messiah in the nations today, as it was for ancient Israel and also for modern Israel, leading up to the return of the Lord.

The LORD is exalted, for He dwells on high; He has filled Zion with justice and righteousness. ***Wisdom and knowledge will be the stability of your times****, and the* **strength of salvation***. The fear of the LORD is His treasure*...

The sinners in Zion are afraid; fearfulness has seized the hypocrites*:*

"Who among us shall dwell with the devouring fire? **Who among us shall dwell with everlasting burnings?"**

He who walks righteously *and speaks uprightly, he who despises the gain of oppressions, who gestures with his hands, refusing bribes*...**bread will be given him***, and* **his water will be sure.**

Your eyes will see the King in His beauty*; they will see the land that is very far off* (Isa. 33:5-6, 14-17).

In verse 6, the Hebrew word for "stability" is "*emunah*," which means faithfulness, or reliability.

In the phrase, "the strength of salvation," the Hebrew word for "strength," is "*hosen*" (Strong's H2633). It is defined as: treasure, riches, strength, wealth. So this word is more than "strength," for it also implies treasures and riches.

The Hebrew word for "salvation" is "*yeshu'ot*," (Strong's H3444). It is defined as "salvation, deliverance, health, welfare, or prosperity."

"*Yeshu'ot*" is the plural form of the same word that was our Lord's Name: "*Yeshua*," or in English, "Jesus." Remember the Angel's word at His conception: "*For He shall SAVE His people*."

We could translate this verse like this: "*Wisdom and Knowledge will keep you faithfully, reliably, and in stability, during these unstable times in which we live; Wisdom and Knowledge will also give you the strength and the riches of God's salvations, deliverances, provisions, blessings, and treasures.*"

And then the Lord adds, "***The fear of the LORD is His treasure.***"

In this passage, we see the Lord filling Zion with His justice and righteousness and granting Wisdom and Knowledge to His people who fear Him. This **wisdom** and **knowledge** will **stabilize His people during the worst of times. Fear will not grip them because they fear the Lord.** Knowing Him will keep us stable in the coming days.

He says, "The fear of the Lord is His treasure" – this gift is most valuable in His eyes, the gift of fearing Him. This treasure "purchases" our protection, stability, safety, and promises. As we saw from the Hebrew, "the strength of salvation," means the power and wealth to be delivered out of a dangerous situation.

But *the sinners in Zion are afraid, and **fear has gripped the hypocrites**.* **This is the other side of fear.** Those hypocrites who pay lip service, but do not fear the Lord, will fear His judgments.

Why do they ask, "Who can dwell with everlasting burnings?"

Are they speaking of the fire of hell? No, they are referring to the unbearable fire of the Lord's holiness and jealousy. Hypocrites cannot bear the heat of God's fire: the demanding, jealous fire of His love, which they have hidden from. Now, they are in terror from the **oven of His judgments** (see Mal.3:2).

In the next chapter, you will read a personal testimony from one who has seen and experienced the **fire of the Lord** on the Day of Judgment. And we will understand Isaiah's question: *"Who can dwell in everlasting burnings?"* His fire will neither destroy us nor our works if we walked in obedience and in the Fear of the Lord during our lives on earth.

Those who fear the Lord receive a promise that even in famine and war, the Lord will give them their daily bread, and their water is sure. This is an encouraging end-time promise for us. We will not fear the terror by night. The plague will not come near our dwelling. Our bread and our water are certain. Praise His faithfulness!

Examples for Our Sakes

Paul warned the church that the punishments which befell Israel were written as a warning and example to us in the New Covenant (see 1Cor.10:6). If we look at each of these cases, we see that the people involved did not fear the Lord. The Fear of the Lord would have saved them in every case.

*Then Nadab and Abihu, the sons of Aaron, each took his censer and put fire in it, put incense on it, and offered **profane fire** before the Lord, **which He had not commanded them**. So fire went out from the Lord and devoured them, and they died before the Lord* (Lev.10:1-2).

This offering of "strange fire, i.e., unauthorized fire, serves as an urgent warning. The fiery death that fell upon the two sons of Aaron **brought great fear to Moses, Aaron,** the **Levites,** and all **the people of Israel.** The High Priest was under a higher accountability before the

Lord than the Levites. These two sons of the High Priest went **presumptuously** into the Holy Place and offered fire that was **not authorized** or prescribed by the Lord. They were instantly consumed with fire that fell from Heaven. Presumption is the opposite of the Fear of the Lord.

The second example is the harsh punishment that befell Israel, due to unbelief, grumbling, and disobedience. **If they had feared the Lord**, not one of these sins and consequential punishments would have taken place.

*Because all these men...have **put Me to the test now these ten times**, and have not heeded My voice, they certainly shall not see the land of which I swore to their fathers, nor shall any of those who rejected Me see it...**the carcasses of those who have complained against Me shall fall in this wilderness*** (Nu.14:22-23, 29a).

Here are some of the tests Israel failed:
- Impatience as Moses tarried too long on the mountain
- Committing idolatry with the golden calf at the foot of the holy mountain
- Lack of trust concerning food and water
- Unwillingness to go into battle with gigantic inhabitants
- Rebellion against God's chosen leadership
- Murmuring and complaining about the hardships
- Ingratitude, forgetting all that the Lord had done to bring them out of bondage

Our final example involves treating the holy Presence of God in a casual manner. Uzzah meant well, but **he did not fear the Lord**. Perhaps as a Levite, he felt it was no big deal to touch the ark, and he felt he was helping God in this way.

*They set the ark of God on a new cart and brought it from the house of Abinadab, which was on the hill. Uzzah and Ahio, sons of Abinadab, were guiding the new cart with the ark of God on it, and Ahio was walking in front of it...When they came to the threshing floor of Nacon, **Uzzah** reached out and **took hold of the ark of God**, because **the oxen stumbled. The Lord's anger burned against Uzzah because of his irreverent act**; therefore **God struck him down** and **he died** there beside the ark of God* (2Sam.6:3-7, NIV).

The Lord's swift punishment upon Uzzah frightened and angered David so much that he refused to bring the ark up to Jerusalem. He had not understood God's requirements for transporting the holy Ark of the Covenant, which was the very habitation of the Lord's glory. He had not consulted the Levites. Later, he did it God's way, with glorious results.

It is vital that we handle God's glory with **reverence** and in His prescribed way. The Fear of the Lord will protect us from stewarding the Presence and glory of God with our own man-made ideas and programs.

Judgment on Hypocrisy

Hypocrisy is the opposite of the Fear of the Lord. If you fear Him, you realize His eyes see all that you do, think, and say, even your secret thoughts. A hypocrite puts on an exterior demeanor that is false. It looks good on the outside, but this is the opposite of what is happening inside his heart. Therefore, hypocrisy is the opposite of fearing the Lord and will be punished most severely. The Lord gives several sobering warnings.

*For nothing is secret that will not be revealed, nor anything hidden that will not be known and come to light. Therefore **whatever you have spoken in the dark will be heard in the light**, and what you have spoken in the ear in inner rooms will be proclaimed on the housetops* (Lk.8:17,12:3).

*For the master of that servant will come on a day when he is not looking for him and at an hour that he is not aware, and will cut him in two and **appoint him his portion with the hypocrites**. There shall be weeping and gnashing of teeth* (Mt.24:51).

*For the heart is **deceitful** above all things, and desperately wicked; who can know it?* (Jer. 17:9).

Ananias and Sapphira Did Not Fear God

But a certain man named Ananias, with Sapphira his wife, sold a possession. And he kept back part of the proceeds, his wife also being aware of it, and brought a certain part and laid it at the apostles' feet.
But Peter said, "Ananias, why has Satan filled your heart to lie to the Holy Spirit and keep back part of the price of the land for yourself? While it remained, was it not your own? And after it was sold, was

it not in your own control? Why have you conceived this thing in your heart? ***You have not lied to men but to God.***"

Then Ananias, hearing these words, fell down and breathed his last. ***So great fear came upon all those who heard these things.*** *And the young men arose and wrapped him up, carried him out, and buried him.*

Now it was about three hours later when his wife came in, not knowing what had happened. And Peter answered her, "Tell me whether you sold the land for so much?"

She said, "Yes, for so much."

Then Peter said to her, "How is it that you have agreed together to test the Spirit of the Lord? Look, the feet of those who have buried your husband are at the door, and they will carry you out." Then immediately she fell down at his feet and breathed her last. And the young men came in and found her dead, and carrying her out, buried her by her husband. ***So great fear came upon all the church and upon all who heard these things*** (Acts 5:1-11).

This warning gives me a profound fear of the Lord and a determination not to lie, or walk in hypocrisy. It is easy to lie without realizing it. These were professing Christians – we must realize that these warnings are directed at those who claim to be members of the body of Messiah.

If this Christian couple had feared the Lord or had even **known the Lord** at all, they would have realized that lying to Peter was insanely foolish and dangerous. When we fear the Lord, we know He hears every thought, every private conversation. We know there is nothing hidden from His eyes. Ananias and Sapphira seemed to have no understanding that the Holy One knew everything about their activities. The Fear of the Lord would have saved their lives.

When we speak to people "privately," we never know to whom the Lord might reveal the secrets of our heart. I am terrified of hypocrisy in my life, and I ask the Lord to search my heart from time to time, making sure I am transparent in public and in private.

The Lord warned us that every word we speak "in secret" will be exposed publicly, before earth and Heaven. I still have not walked in the fullness of this healthy fear. I still say things I would be horrified to hear later, broadcast across Heaven. This means I am not walking fully in the Fear of the Lord. I'm telling you this so you know we all need this foundational attribute in our hearts. If we will repent before Him privately, the Lord is gracious to cleanse and forgive us, and He will not expose us publicly, nor before Heaven's courts.

There is a Healthy Fear

Some years ago, I attended a conference where prophet Sadhu Sundar Selvaraj was speaking. He was teaching about Ananias and Sapphira. Although I had read this story many times, the tangible Fear of the Lord fell upon us that night, as he preached in the power of the Spirit. I had been a believer for 34 years, yet I had almost never felt this fear before. Even when the Manifest Presence of the Lord overshadowed me in 1993, I didn't feel this exact type of fear.

As I listened to these warnings, I felt afraid of the Lord and almost questioned my salvation. I didn't doubt that I was saved, but I felt vulnerable and undone. It felt like the ceiling was gone, the sky was rolled back, and I was exposed before a righteous and holy God. I felt His glance was penetrating every secret motive of my heart.

I didn't feel convicted of any particular hypocrisy in my life, but I felt a general sense of anxiety and uncleanness inside. I wondered who could stand under this scrutiny. My body trembled and my soul wanted to run and hide. Even though I loved the Lord, I wanted to crawl away somewhere, but there was nowhere to go. This is what the Manifested Fear of the Lord feels like. You know it won't help to run away, and that in Heaven, you won't be able to hide anywhere. You will just stand there and take it because there is no option.

In a way, the Fear of the Lord is a terrible feeling, but it's not the same as the condemnation of the enemy. They both feel uncomfortable, but the difference is this:

Condemnation feels like, *"I hate you, you revolting piece of slime. I remember every vile thing you ever thought or did or said, and I'm playing them back before the throne of God every day, so He realizes how disgusting you are."*

The Fear of the Lord feels like, *"Yes, you are naked, yes you are dust, yes you are vulnerable. Yes, your heart must become as pure as crystal water. But I love you and I will make you acceptable, and I am able to present you blameless on That Day."*

As I waited for Sadhu to bring us the reassurance we all needed, I thought, "What if there is still hypocrisy in my heart and I haven't discovered it?"

I knew that deception is deceptive.

He did not require everyone to kneel down as he brought us to a place of public repentance and soul-searching. Rather, he said, "Those of you that want to kneel down and search your hearts, do so now."

While we were kneeling for quite some time, he announced, "This is the word that the Lord Jesus is speaking to me right now: *"Hypocrites will be judged...hypocrites will be judged."*

We were all thinking, "O Lord, please don't let it be me!"

I became so worried that something bad was in my heart that the Holy Spirit said to me, *"Trust Me."* Then I felt reassured and just rested in His presence, knowing He would certainly convict me if something needed to be addressed.

There is a balance in our response to this warning. The Lord loves us! He is able to keep us from stumbling and to present us blameless before the Father on that day! (see Jude 24).

Chapter 9
The Judgment Seat of Messiah

*And now, Israel, what does the Lord your God require of you
But to fear the Lord your God
To walk in all His ways and to love Him
To serve the Lord your God with all your heart
And with all your soul.
Deuteronomy 10:12*

There are several types and meanings of "judgment," mentioned throughout the Bible. Let's look at how this word is applied in its various contexts. The word "Judgment" is used 293 times in the Old Testament and 79 times in the New Testament.

In Hebrew, the word for judgment is *"mish'pat,"* and in Strong's Concordance (H4941), it is partially defined this way:

"From H8199; properly, a **verdict** (favorable or unfavorable) **pronounced judicially**, especially **a sentence or formal decree**…"

In different Bible verses, it is used in the following ways:
- judgment
- act of deciding a case
- place, court, seat of judgment
- process, procedure, litigation (before judges)
- case, cause (presented for judgment)
- sentence, decision (of judgment)
- execution (of judgment)
- time (of judgment)
- justice, right, rectitude (attributes of God or man)

As I began to research the Judgment Seat of Messiah, I was shocked to find that virtually every mention of the word "judgment" in the Old Testament is referring to the Lord's judgments **in the earth**, or **upon the earth,** upon individuals, nations, or people groups living on the earth at any given time.

For God's people Israel, His chosen leaders in each generation would **teach**, **enforce** and **execute** His laws, decrees, and punishments for sin. If another wicked nation was worthy of judgment, the Lord would tell His Israelite prophets, who would then declare the Word of the Lord over Babylon, Egypt, etc.

This word, *"judgment,"* was almost never used to speak of a future judgment of individual human souls after their death. Out of 293 mentions, I only found a few cases where it may be implying a future Day of Judgment for souls or for nations. These few cases were only found in the Psalms and a few times in Isaiah. At other times, the prophetic writings indirectly speak of future judgments, but they are mostly speaking of judgments that fall upon cities or nations, rather than upon individuals (in the future), standing before a Heavenly Throne. Here are some Old Testament samples that describe a future judgment:

But the Lord shall endure forever; ***He has prepared His throne for judgment. He shall judge the world in righteousness****, and He shall administer judgment for the peoples in uprightness* (Ps.9:7-8).

This throne could possibly refer to the final Judgment Throne, but He is still speaking of ruling over the nations of the earth.

For thrones are set there for judgment*, the thrones of the house of David* (Ps.122:5).

These refer to the governmental structures (thrones) that will exist under the future theocratic government of Israel. King Yeshua, as the prophesied Son of David, will be granted the Kingdom over the nations of the Millennial earth and will reign from Jerusalem. In the Millennial Kingdom, David himself (in his resurrected body) will be granted to rule the Kingdom of Israel, and he will rule under the authority of the King of Kings, Lord Yeshua the Messiah.

Near the end of the Lord Yeshua's earthly ministry, He told His 12 Jewish Apostles that Israel's leadership will be entrusted to them; they will be granted to sit on 12 thrones, **judging (ruling) the 12 tribes of Israel**. I believe they will be governing the 12 tribes of Israel under David's authority over the Millennial Kingdom of Israel. See supporting texts below, two of which are from the New Testament.

*a. So Jesus said to them, "Assuredly I say to you, that in the regeneration, when the Son of Man sits on the throne of His glory, you who have followed Me will **also sit on twelve thrones, judging the twelve tribes of Israel*** (Mt.19:28).

b. *"...that you may eat and drink at My table **in My kingdom, and sit on thrones judging the twelve tribes of Israel**"* (Lk.22:30).

c. *Of the increase of His government and peace there will be no end, **upon the throne of David and over His kingdom**, to order it and establish it **with judgment and justice** from that time forward, even forever. The zeal of the Lord of hosts will perform this* (Isa.9:7).

Apart from these rare cases, "Judgment" in the Old Testament consisted of the Lord entrusting His appointed leaders, judges, kings, and prophets, to govern and rule over His people's morals, disputes, crimes, and disobedience on earth. **The judges would judge each case according to the Law of the Lord.** At times, these Israelite leaders also pronounced judgments over gentile nations for their bad behavior or their wicked spiritual or governmental policies. This was earthly justice, from Heaven's laws, enforced by God's chosen human leaders.

The New Testament Revelation of Judgment

As I continued my Bible study into the New Testament, I was actually shocked again. I saw that as soon as Lord Yeshua began His public ministry, He immediately began to teach about eternal judgment (punishment and eternal rewards) on individual human souls.

He spoke about it often, and it was always about facing a Heavenly Judge after we have lived our lives and left our bodies. In His teachings, we see ourselves (our souls) standing before the Great Judgment Seat of God, being (potentially) reproached and condemned, or praised and rewarded, depending on our lives on earth.

I'll provide examples below so that you can see the Word of the Lord. In the cases where the Lord warns of condemnation, He is responding to many "common" wrongdoings, heart attitudes, and sins we have done on earth. The Lord tells us that even some of these "little things" are a serious offense to the Father, and they will land us in hell fire (His words). In some cases, He is condemning cities and even the generation in which He lived.

*But I say to you that whoever is angry with his brother without a cause shall be in danger of **the judgment**. And whoever says to his brother, 'Raca!' shall be in danger of **the council**. But whoever says, 'You fool!' shall be in danger of **hell fire*** (Mt.5:22).

*For with what judgment you judge, **you will be judged**; and with the measure you use, it will be measured back to you* (Mt.7:2).

*Assuredly, I say to you, it will be more tolerable for the land of Sodom and Gomorrah in **the day of judgment** than for that city!* (Mt.10:15).

*But I say to you that for **every idle word** men may speak, they will **give account** of it in the **day of judgment*** (Mt.12:36).

*The men of Nineveh will rise up in **the judgment with this generation** and condemn it, because they repented at the preaching of Jonah; and indeed a greater than Jonah is here* (Mt.12:41).

*For the Father judges no one, but has committed **all judgment to the Son*** (Jn.5:22).

*"Most assuredly, I say to you, he who hears My word and believes in Him who sent Me has everlasting life, and shall **not come into judgment**, but has passed from death into life* (Jn.5:24).

*…and has given Him authority to **execute judgment** also, because He is the Son of Man* (Jn.5:27).

The Judgment Seat

We see that this term, "the Judgment Seat," appears about 12 times in the New Testament. Its normal usage is about human rulers, such as Caesar or Pontius Pilate, seated on a "throne of government," or a "Judgment Seat."

In Greek, the word for "judgment seat" is *"bema."* Strong's Concordance (G968) defines it as: "judgment seat; throne; to set one's foot on." The primary biblical usage is:
- a raised place mounted by steps
- a platform, tribune
- of the official seat of a judge
- of the judgment seat of Christ

Here are a few examples where this word is used for human governors and kings:

*While he was sitting on **the judgment seat**, his wife sent to him, saying, "Have nothing to do with that just Man, for I have suffered many things today in a dream because of Him"* (Mt. 27:19).

*When Pilate therefore heard that saying, he brought Jesus out and sat down in the **judgment seat** in a place that is called* The *Pavement, but in Hebrew, Gabbatha* (Jn.19:13).

*So on a set day Herod, arrayed in royal apparel, sat on his **throne** [bema,] and gave an oration to them* (Act.12:21).

So Paul said, "I stand at **Caesar's judgment seat**, where I ought to be judged. To the Jews I have done no wrong, as you very well know (Act. 25:10).

The Judgment Seat of Messiah

Paul was well-acquainted with the term, "*bema,*" and he himself had been on trial a number of times, before an unjust judge on his "throne of government." Paul was given exceptional revelation about a unique, heavenly Judgment Seat, before which **believers in Yeshua** will stand and **give an account** of their lives and motives.

Paul had seen Gallio's and Caesar's judgment seats on earth. But the Lord showed him what the **eternal Judgment Seat of Messiah** will look like and what He will ask of us when we stand before Him. Believers are not judged at the same time, nor under the same conditions, as unbelievers. It is a different Judgment event, as many Scriptures will verify. As you see below, Paul is writing to believers: "Why do you judge your brother?"

*But why do you judge your brother? Or why do you show contempt for your brother? We shall **all** stand before the **Judgment Seat of Christ**...Then each of us shall **give account** of himself to God* (Rom.14:10,12).

What does it mean to "give account?" First, Paul says, *"Why do you judge your brother?"*

This means if we judge our fellow believers, we ourselves will be under a stricter judgment, since we are guilty of the same things, and because only God has the right to judge anyone.

"Giving account" also means that the Lord had assignments for each of us. He has a scroll with our name on it, which we were meant to fulfill. He will ask us to account for what we did and did not do. If we see something in our scroll that we had not known or done, we will feel inexpressible pain and regret. We cannot protest, "But Lord, I had no idea I was supposed to do that work."

He will let us know that if we had cared enough to press in and to seek Him, He would have revealed it, but it was not given automatically to us. The Lord is just and fair, and we will not be able to say, "That's not fair." We will know He is right. He is the very definition and embodiment of Justice and Fairness.

We are told in Scripture that the Lord has "books" of the records of our lives. He will open the books and we will look at our lives (see Dan.7:10, Ps.139:16, Ps.40:7). This is scary, to be honest. But if we are diligent to keep short accounts with the Lord, we will not have any painful surprises on that Day.

We will also give an account for how well we used our gifts and how much we shared them with others. There are many heart qualities we will also have to give account for. We cannot cover all the aspects of this Judgment here since none of us has walked through it. But this chapter is given to help us prepare.

Does the Believer Receive Eternal Rewards at this Judgment?

*For we must all appear before the judgment seat of Christ, that each one **may receive the things done in the body**, according to what he has done, **whether good or bad** (2Cor.5:10).*

Notice that it says, "whether good or bad." This implies that we will receive rewards for the good that we did, and we will either lose rewards, endure chastisement, or suffer "loss," for the bad we have done in this life. **The Judgment Seat for believers is not meant for eternal punishment, but for evaluation.** However, if we suffer loss or chastisement, it will be painful to us, and we will suffer agonizing regret.

*Each one will receive his **own reward** according to his **own labor**. If anyone builds on this foundation with **gold, silver, precious stones**, [OR] **wood, hay, straw**, each one's work will become clear; for the Day will declare it, because it will be **revealed by fire**; and the **fire will test** each one's work. If anyone's work which he has built on it **endures**, he will receive a **reward**.*

*If anyone's work is burned, **he will suffer loss**; but **he himself will be saved**, yet so as **through fire** (1Cor.3:8-15).*

What are Wood, Hay, and Straw?

What does the Lord mean by "wood, hay, and straw," which are burned in a moment? All that we did with selfish motives, for our own benefit. This could include the desire for financial gain, and using the ministry to attain it; making a name for ourselves or our ministry, or just to feel good about ourselves; and other things which did not bring the people into a more intimate and holy relationship with the Lord. It could also apply to activities or plans which were not initiated by the Spirit of God, but which we planned out of our own wishes, without checking with the Lord if this was pleasing to Him. The things He didn't call us to do will not endure the fire.

What does it mean that our work is burned? What does it mean to be saved, **but as through the fire?** I have heard and read a number of testimonies from different teachers, pastors, and prophets, who have all been given a similar revelatory experience from the Lord. One of them I know personally. They have been taken into the future, and have seen believers before the Judgment Throne of Messiah. In this case below, one leader shared this sobering testimony.

A Glimpse of That Day

I heard a respected teacher and prophet share the following testimony about the Judgment Seat of Messiah. He was taken into the future and saw a certain Judgment scene taking place. This was not the judgment for "regular believers," but this judgment was particularly for leaders in the Body of Messiah. The prophet said that previously, he had also been shown the Judgment Seat for "regular believers," and he understood that this judgment for leaders was much more intense. Leaders were much more accountable.

This judgment applied to **all leaders**, not only pastors who have a church. Anyone who leads or teaches other believers are "leaders" in the Lord's eyes.

He saw a group of people waiting to be called, and one particular leader was called to give an account to the Lord. The prophet did not know this man's name on earth, and he did not want to know his name. The Lord asked the man two questions.

The **first question**: *"Where was your heart?"* (Meaning, where was his heart during his time on earth).

At this moment, the Lord turned and looked the prophet in the eye, and said, *"I do not look at anything outward, ever. I look at the heart."*

The Lord continued speaking to the leader.

"You left your first love. You led people away from the will of My Father, to your own will. You worked directly against the Spirit of God. You established your own kingdom. I called you to get people to Me, by you getting to Me, and being an example."

The man was weeping uncontrollably and gnashing his teeth in regret. He was longing to come back to earth and re-live it. It was too late.

The **next question**: *"Let's look at your works."*

All was burned up, and here is how it happened:

It's as if the Lord opened Himself up, and the man stepped into the OVEN – the consuming fire that God, in Christ, **is**.

The prophet was allowed to feel what that brother felt, for a moment. Before he shared what he felt in the Lord's fire, he told us that many years ago, he had been taken in a prophetic experience to the lower regions of hell, where only demonic spirits were – they had been confined there, since the flood (see 2Pet.2:4, Jude 1:6). No humans were in that lower realm. There was darkness and fire with no light. He had felt the heat in that dreadful place. But in comparison, when this brother stepped into Yeshua's fire, the prophet told us: **"God is a fire like no other fire. Hell has no comparison to Him."**

The prophet was allowed to experience a little bit of this fire. Such was the intensity of the fire of the Lord that he (the prophet) wished he had never been born. And so did the brother who was being judged.

He said, "Everything was burned up. His soul was saved, but everything was burned up."

The prophet then explained, "We are called to get to Him here (on earth) and to **be** His possession, and to **be** an example of what it means to be wholeheartedly in love with Jesus. We're to be examples, first and foremost. Not preachers. Examples. Not teachers. Examples. Not to mimic words or echo words – examples. Wholeheartedly given to the Lord, the Lord taking hold of us. Possessing us. To proclaim Him and nothing else." [End of testimony.]

This is what Paul meant when he said: *If anyone's work is burned,* **he will suffer loss;** *but* **he himself will be saved,** *yet so as* **through fire** (1Cor.3:8-15). It would be like you are dashing out of a house on fire, with no time to take your possessions with you. You just get by with your life, but you lose everything. You can take nothing with you.

What Works are Gold, Silver, and Precious Stones?

What does it mean to build on the foundation with gold, silver, and precious stones? These are the most valuable building materials, which represent our works that have **lasting spiritual benefit** for the Lord's plans, and for His people's hearts, as measured by Kingdom standards.

I believe what the Lord calls "gold" is that which was birthed out of **His initiative, by His Spirit rather than our own ideas**, and works that were **born through intimacy with Him**. He invests Himself in the work He has initiated, if we are doing a work that came from His heart.

For example, as a songwriter, I have learned that when a song is birthed out of my intimate relationship with the Lord, the listeners get closer to the Lord when they hear it. It is not a song that I just decided to write. It is not entertainment, but is rather, a vehicle to bring them into deeper communion with His heart.

"Gold" is when the Lord Yeshua appoints a task or goal that He purposed for us, and we simply do it, drawing on His wisdom, help, and strength to do it. We were not doing our own thing, and just hoping He would join us. No, we need to **join Him**. This work will change lives, one heart at a time, and this is precious building material to the Lord. Not necessarily large crowds. He told me this Himself: *"I measure success one heart at a time."* This was a great comfort to me.

The Lord will show you which of His good works He is initiating in your life. You were born for His specific assignments that fit you perfectly. And He is waiting for you. **Let Him lead the steps of your dance.** He is the Bridegroom. This precious building material can withstand the fire and suffer no loss.

Mike Bickle's Life-Changing Testimony

Pastor Mike Bickle (Director of International House of Prayer in Kansas City, MO) has shared a gripping testimony from his life, many years ago. He was shown what many believers will face, when they stand before the Judgment Seat, unprepared for the Lord's evaluation. Mike has shared this testimony a number of times over the years because it was an unforgettable warning, which would set the course of his life. He doesn't want anyone to have to live through that experience when it will be too late to go back and change things. It is quite similar to the other prophet's testimony shared above. But it is good to have at least two witnesses to this reality. It will help us never to have to face such terrible grief, regret, and loss.

When Mike was a young man, in October 1978, he had a dream. He had been sleeping in bed, but he suddenly found himself kneeling before the throne of Jesus Christ. He didn't know how he got there. He even wondered if he had died. He was just there, face to face with the Lord. The Lord said to him, *"You are saved, but your life was wasted."*

Mike knew he had been pressing in to know the Lord, during that season of this life. He had been reading missionary biographies and doing his best to walk with the Lord. He wanted to protest that the Lord's assessment of his life couldn't be true.

But a thought rose up strongly in him, from the Holy Spirit: *"It is impossible to manipulate the Man Christ Jesus."* He realized he could not change the Lord's opinion about his life. Then, thinking that he had died, he desperately wanted to go back and do things better. He cried out, "Can I have another chance?"

Then the thought came to him, *"It is appointed unto man to die once, then comes the judgment* (Heb.9:27).

So he knew He couldn't change the Lord's opinion of his life, and he knew he couldn't go back to do it again. This was the final verdict on his life. He wept with a profound sense of loss and regret.

When he came out of the experience, he was not in bed, where he had started. He was kneeling, weeping profusely, and his T-shirt was wet with his tears.

As the days and weeks went by after that life-shattering experience, the Lord began to communicate with him about why He had allowed Mike to feel such terrible sorrow and regret. The Lord showed him that having this experience "now" would cause him to live in such a way as to **not have any regret** on the Last Day. It was a warning, so this terrible event would never take place in the future. He shares it so none of us will ever have to face that appalling, irreversible verdict: *"Saved, but your life was wasted."*

Mike writes: "A life without regret is based on seeking to walk out the **first commandment** with a spirit of faith and obedience. That is what Jesus wants most in us. What matters most about our life is what Jesus will think, when our eyes meet. I fear regret more than anything else in my life. I pray, 'Lord, shock me now, do not wait until then.'" [End of testimony]

The first and greatest commandment is: *"Love the Lord your God with all your heart, all your soul, all your strength and all your mind "* (see Mt.22:35-40, Deut.6:4).

Boldness on the Day of Judgment

*Love has been perfected among us in this: that we may have **boldness in the day of judgment;** because as He is, so are we in this world* (1Jn.4:17).

The Apostle John walked in the love of the Lord. He wasn't always this way in his youth, but as he grew older, and became a spiritual father to many, love was perfected in John. He could truly say, *"As He is, so are we in this world."* John is telling us that when love is perfected in us, we can face the Day of Judgment without fear or regret. We can boldly stand before the Lord because His love will have been made perfect in us, if we allow Him.

A question that a certain prophet heard the Lord ask at the Judgment Throne was: *"Did you learn to love?"*

I pray we can all answer that question, "Yes, Lord, I did."

If we can't answer "yes" now, how about we start working on it, before that day?

Eternal Rewards are the Lord's Response to our Lives

*The Son of Man will come...He will **reward each according to his works*** (Mt.16:27).

Remember that we are not saved by our works. Salvation is the free gift of God, for all who will believe, receive, and obey the Lord Yeshua the Messiah. His blood has made atonement for our sins and by this, His virtue and free gift, we receive salvation.

Eternal rewards are the Lord's response to **how we responded to His atoning sacrifice** – to His love and generosity, to His commandments. If we please Him in our loving responses to Him, He is pleased to grant us eternal rewards, based on what we have done (with motives that please Him). It makes Him happy to give His children rewards on that Day.

*The Lord...will both bring to light the **hidden things** of darkness and reveal the counsels of the hearts. Then each one's **praise** will come from **God*** (1Cor.4:5).

The depths of our hearts are known to the Lord. He will shine His light on our heart. If our hearts do not condemn us, we have confidence; then our praise will come from God.

*For if our heart condemns us, **God is greater than our heart**, and knows all things.*
*Beloved, **if our heart does not condemn us, we have confidence toward God**. And **whatever we ask we receive from Him**, because we keep His commandments and **do those things that are pleasing in His sight*** (1Jn.3:20-22).

*And whoever gives one of these little ones only a **cup of cold water** in the name of a disciple, assuredly, I say to you, he shall by no means lose his **reward**. (Mt.10:42)*

Our acts of kindness and generosity to the poor, lonely, and hurting are very important to the Lord. He will not miss one of our acts of kindness, and He will generously reward it, far beyond what we would deserve.

But remember that these deeds must be done before the eyes of the Lord only, and not before the eyes of men. If our motive is to be praised by people for our good deeds, we have lost our reward. So we must constantly guard the motives for which we do acts of kindness and charity.

*Take heed that you do not do your charitable deeds before men, **to be seen by them**. Otherwise you have **no reward** from your Father...When you do a charitable deed, do not sound a trumpet before you as the hypocrites do...they have their reward...Your charitable deed may be **in secret**; and your Father who **sees in secret** will Himself **reward you*** (Mt. 6:1-4).

The Lord's rewards cannot be imagined. How generous is His heart! Something so small we did years ago and forgot about it, the Lord will remind us.

He will say, *"Do you remember when you got that lady groceries, as she was trying to pay her bill at checkout?"*

And you will say, "No, I don't remember that, Lord."

And He will say, *"Well, I remember. This is my reward for that act of kindness."*

Or He will say, *"Do you remember when that strange man came into church, and just sat there through the whole service, with no one talking to him? And you went up to him afterward and offered to take him out for coffee?"*

And you will say, "Yes, I remember that, Lord. I felt bad for him. Everyone else was going out to lunch with their friends, but he was just sitting there."

And He will say, *"I remember it too. You cheered him up so much, and you told Him about Me over that cup of coffee. This is your reward for that act of love for a stranger."*

Beloved, may all our conversations with the Lord, when we stand before His Judgment Seat, be those of love and honor, and never of fear or reproach. This concludes our teaching on the Judgment Seat of Messiah. AMEN.

There is no fear in love; but perfect love casts out fear, because fear involves torment. But he who fears has not been made perfect in love (1Jn.4:18).

Chapter 10
Warfare in the Spiritual Realm

When you go to war in your land
Against the enemy who oppresses you
Then you shall sound an alarm with the trumpets
And you will be remembered before the Lord your God
And you will be saved from your enemies.
Numbers 10:9

There is a powerful spiritual realm that is invisible to our natural eyes, but it is as real as what we see. It is not the purpose of this book to teach extensively on the realm of the demonic, but we must explore this realm since we are learning to overcome fear.

Emotion and Chemistry

"Fear" is a negative human emotion, which signals our brains and bodies to release a unique chemical into the bloodstream. All of our bodies' chemistry was created by God, and this chemical was meant to be released when we feel the emotion of fear. If we were continually in fear and producing this chemical often, it would put our heart health at risk. But it is helpful to us if we find ourselves in true danger.

However, "Fear" is also an evil spirit or a group of spirits, with the ability to manipulate both our natural chemistry and our emotions. We'll return to the spiritual battle in a moment.

Normally, our natural human fear is triggered when we find ourselves in a dangerous or threatening situation. The many examples in our world are evident: car accidents; personal crime; fires; natural disasters, terror attacks, and other factors. Our fear releases a chemical called "adrenaline," which gives us the energy to either escape or to confront (fight) the danger before us. This effect of adrenaline is commonly called "fight or flight." It affects our body by raising our heart rate and blood pressure.

In these emergency cases, it is hard to "calm down." In crisis mode, our bodies are designed **not** to be calm and tranquil. However, I have heard many testimonies (and you may also have heard these) where a believer was suddenly thrust into a crisis, and terror and chaos surrounded them. The other people at the scene (of the accident, crime, explosion, fire, etc.) were responding in the natural way, with fear and panic. However, believers have testified that in the midst of terror and chaos, a supernatural, peace settled upon them. It was like a blanket of the Holy Spirit resting upon a child of God. His nearness, His Presence, and His sovereignty (Him being in control over the situation) settled upon them.

This Presence makes it impossible to feel the normal human emotions of panic, terror, desperation, or frantic activity. The Spirit of the Lord has imposed His peace over you, despite the circumstances. People around you begin to feel the peace and calm emanating from you. At that point, **it is possible to think clearly** and begin to take steps to help people get through the situation. This peace that passes all understanding is a fruit of the Holy Spirit, and it will serve us well in the perilous times ahead.

Demonic Attacks

There are Christians in certain theological views, who do not even believe that demonic activity is real and threatening to both believers and unbelievers alike. They say we are "giving too much credit to the enemy," if we attribute various forms of attacks – evil visitations, hallucinations, physical attacks, illness, terror, nightmares, unexplainable phenomena – to Satan and his evil minions. They say this is not to be "credited" to demonic activity. They offer other sources and treat the problems in "natural" ways, though they cannot be explained. I realize that these things can also occur by natural causes, and not all are from the devil. But plenty of them are and must be faced in a biblical and decisive way.

This is like an ostrich burying her head in the sand, and saying, "There is no enemy that can harm me because I cannot see him!"

This is unbiblical theology. You only have to read the New Testament to see the massive number of references that our Lord Yeshua made to the power of Satan, and that the Apostle Paul made to the enemy's power, limited authority, and influence. The Lord Himself cast out demons many times in the New Testament, and only a small number of His total works were recorded in the Bible. The Apostle John tells us that if we tried to document all the works of Yeshua, during his brief time on earth, "the world could not contain the number of books that would be written!" (see John 21:25).

Not only did the Lord and His Apostles verify that demonic activity and power were real, but they also commanded us to fight the same spiritual battles as they did. If Satan and his demons have no more power, since the time when Yeshua was crucified and resurrected, why did the Apostles write that we are *"not wrestling against flesh and blood, but against rulers of the darkness of this age, against spiritual hosts of wickedness in the heavenly places"?* (see Eph.6:12).

Peter also warned us about the real threat of this enemy: *Be sober, be vigilant, because your adversary the devil walks about like a roaring lion, seeking whom he may devour (1Pet 5:8).*

The Lord's death and resurrection stripped Satan of his authority to possess mankind and to own their souls forever. We could never have paid for our own sins. Our condemnation was certain, and death and hell would have been our prison for eternity. The Lord overcame sin, death, the grave, and hell's power over us. Yeshua took back what the enemy had stolen at the Fall. Bless His Name for rescuing us!

However, this victory is not automatically enforced on the earth in this present age. Only believers who **exercise the authority** the Lord purchased for us on the cross and through His resurrection, will defeat the enemy's attacks, deceptions, and strategies. To the extent that believers sit back and do not exercise their God-given authority in the Name and the blood of Yeshua, then Satan will continue to operate as if "nothing happened" that would bother his plans. He will proceed with every manner of calculated evil.

Authority Over Evil Spirits

For those who have received the Lord Yeshua (Jesus) the Messiah as their Savior and Lord, you already know what the Scriptures teach us about our authority, regarding evil spirits. Consider how many Scriptures assert the authority the Lord has given us:

*Then the seventy returned with joy, saying, "Lord, even **the demons are subject to us in Your name."***

*And He said to them, "I saw Satan fall like lightning from heaven. Behold, **I give you the authority to trample on serpents and scorpions**, and over **all the power of the enemy**, and **nothing shall by any means hurt you*** (Lk.10:17-19).

The Lord's reference to "serpents and scorpions" is more directed towards evil spirits, than to the deadly creatures with their poisonous bites and stings. I believe we also have authority over the poisonous animals, but this authority is primarily meant to be used against demonic powers of the enemy (Satan).

*Then He appointed twelve, that they might be with Him and that He might send them out **to preach**, and to **have power to heal sicknesses and to cast out demons*** (Mk.3:14-15).

Those whom He sent out to preach, were given not only the gift of clear, articulate speech but were also given **supernatural power** to heal and to cast demons out of demonized people.

*"Heal the sick, cleanse the lepers, raise the dead, **cast out demons**. Freely you have received, freely give"* (Mt.10:8).

These are **commands** from the Lord, not suggestions. "Heal the sick...cast out demons." Surely these commands were not only meant for those few disciples 2,000 years ago. Why wouldn't this instruction apply to all true disciples, even till the end of the age? Why do we feel – why do we FEAR – that we could not walk in this level of power?

Many of us feel incapable, fearing failure, or lack of faith. I am still weak in this area, though I practice warring in the spirit realm in my own numerous battles. Through gaining victories, I am growing more confident. Many times I have faced attacks and confrontations, both in dreams and in real life, where evil powers are coming against me. I have seen the power and authority of Yeshua's Name uncountable times, to my astonishment. He has saved and delivered me from many fearful challenges from the enemy over the past 15 years. When I speak with faith, believing that the evil spirits MUST back off – the authority of His Name and His blood always banishes them.

Let me share several of these battles and subsequent victories from my own life. I had a powerful dream some years ago, which was significant to my understanding of the authority the Lord has given us over evil spirits that cause disease (see Mt.9:32-33, Mk.16:17-18). The following is the life-changing dream I was given:

Deliverance is a Messy Job – My Dream

I was a teacher at a Christian school. They were having a large gathering, a special party for many of the students and teachers.

In one of the larger multi-purpose classrooms where I was working, there was a 14-year old boy who was lying in an upper bunk bed. He was very sick with a high and contagious fever. He was suffering terribly, and the staff just ignored him and went on with the activities of the party. They were eating pizza and were busy with activities.

I went to check on the boy and seeing his condition, I was outraged that his mother had sent him to school like this. I began to call the other teachers to come over and help me take care of the boy. He had been lying in his own cold urine for hours, shivering and too weak to get up and go to the bathroom. When I asked why he had been brought to school like this, one of the teachers said that his mother wanted to get him out of the house because his fever was so contagious, she was afraid that she and the other children at home would catch it and die. So she selfishly left him with us and the other students, who could also catch the disease.

Everyone ignored him, and when I asked them to help me, they said they were afraid of getting sick. Even though I was a little afraid, I was more motivated to help him than worried about getting sick. Finally, with great effort, I convinced a group of teachers to help me clean him up, and his sheets and clothes. Everything was soaked, and he needed some food or liquid. After a lot of work, we got him freshened up, dry and clean, and put him in a fresh bed in a top bunk.

Then everyone immediately began leaving the room to go back to the party, feeling that he was fine now. I knew they wanted to get away from him and continue their activities. I knew instinctively that he was way too sick to be left alone. As I reluctantly started to walk out the door with the others, the poor boy began to vomit all over his fresh sheets. He tried to get up to go to the bathroom, but he was too weak. I called for the others to come back and help me, but they wouldn't; they did not want to deal with it.

Then I saw many demons coming and going from the boy and his sickbed. They were walking out of the room, between 50 and 100 of them, busy with evil and foul assignments concerning this boy; they were just arrogantly coming and going, all with some kind of destructive assignment and purpose.

I spoke up, to cast them out. No one would help me, and all the teachers ignored me. I tried to raise my voice and speak forcefully enough to command them, but because I was asleep in real life, it was hard to talk loudly enough. I opened my mouth and commanded all of these foul, evil demons of disease and infection and death to leave this boy at once, in Yeshua's Name. My voice came out weaker than I had hoped, and I felt inadequate to cast them out. There were so many of them, but **I spoke it with confidence, knowing they HAD to go.**

At first, they seemed to ignore my words, continuing to file out, and to continue their work; I wondered if I had not succeeded. But then I saw that the tallest demon, who seemed to be in charge of the others, stopped and stared at me. He looked like an arrogant hippie from the "Woodstock" era (the late 1960's and early 70's). He started to answer me, stating that they could all ignore me, but my faith was very strong as I continued to stare back at him.

I knew in my heart that despite their initial outward response, **they had to obey me.** After we had stared at each other for a while, he gave up, realizing that he had no choice. He shrugged in defeat and disgust towards me, and immediately, he and the others left the boy, never to return.

The boy was instantly well again, and I began the chore of cleaning up the boy and his bed again from his recent mess. No one helped me. Then I remembered that several years before, I had cast a demon out of his little brother, who had been crippled and ill, and he had been healed. I remembered that I was known to the demons who afflicted this family, as one who rescued and set them free from these besetting spirits. I knew the demons didn't like it, that this was the second time I had driven them out of someone in this family.

Then I woke up and immediately saw the Lord telling His disciples, *"Do not rejoice that the demons are subject to you, but rather, rejoice that your names are written in the Book of Life."* I marveled that they had obeyed me and that their leader had acknowledged me and the authority with which I had spoken to him.

As I lay in bed, reflecting on this dream, I knew that during the time that the head demon and I were staring at each other, he was **acting like he didn't have to obey me** and leave the boy. It had been vital during this staring contest that I **knew** beyond any doubt, that **they had no choice** but to obey and leave. If my faith had weakened, and if I had not stood my ground in my certainty that they had to go, they would not have left. **Part of the victory was connected to my absolute certainty that no matter how long they resisted, they had no choice but to leave.** I knew this was a critical lesson for all of us who might be in the ministry of casting out demons, both now and in the days to come.

Perhaps the other teachers, who didn't want to deal with the boy or his demons, represented the church, which is "too busy" and ill-equipped to confront the demonic powers we are now facing. It is easier to continue life as we have known it than to move into this messy arena of setting people free. However, the time is coming when we will have no choice but to take up our battle stations. [End of dream testimony.]

You also remember my testimony in Chapter 4, when I spiritually fought for my life in that foreign airport at midnight, as **Satan gave me lying symptoms of a heart attack**. The Lord delivered me. In my life at this present time, in terms of healing and delivering others, I am still at a low level of spiritual warfare. Thankfully, there are many brave and obedient spiritual warriors in our time, who are doing the works that our Lord did, just as He said we would (see John 14:12).

The Source of Suffering

Not all sicknesses and infirmities are of demonic origin. It would be a whole chapter to discuss this in-depth. The purpose of this chapter is to strengthen us in overcoming the fear of the demonic realm, concerning healing and deliverance, and to emphasize the authority the Lord has given to us.

If a disease has a natural cause, then it will not be healed by casting out a demon. It must be diagnosed medically and dealt with through prayer, as well as natural healing procedures. For example, if a child falls from a tree and fractures his spine, it is not of demonic origin. The injury must be treated medically, although prayer will make a tremendous difference in the child's recovery.

Let us consider Job for a moment. The most helpful aspect of Job's testimony is that God did not desire to afflict His friend, Job. It was the enemy's hatred and jealousy that thrust an accusation in God's face, and the **Lord was required to answer Satan's challenge**. The Lord could not ignore this challenge, for it went to the very authenticity of Job's devotion to God. Did Job only love the Lord because He was so generous to him? The Lord had to prove His servant's faithfulness and thus, **silence the enemy's accusations**.

It is helpful to know the source of people's suffering. In Job's case, we are clearly told that his suffering was initiated by Satan. There are times when the enemy will go before the Lord and demand to plunder us, to show God our false motives and how quickly we will turn against Him when our possessions, health, safety or families are harmed. May our motives be proven true and faithful in that terrible test. Amen.

Satan demanded to sift Job, to sift Peter, and to sift many beloved children of God in the days to come. The enemy's job description is: to steal, to kill, and to destroy. These scenarios have played out behind-the-scenes, in the heavenly courtroom (see Job1:6-2:8, Lk.22:31-32). The enemy accuses us before God, day and night (see Rev.12:10).

We were made for partnership with the Lord and to pray His will in the earth, as it is in Heaven; we are to petition His throne for every victory in the spiritual realm. He taught us to pray, knowing the schemes of the enemy. We are to use the sword of the Spirit, which is the Word of God, to tear down the enemy's strategies against the saints of the Most High.

The Lord Allows Us to be Tested

*...you have been grieved by various trials, so that the genuineness of **your faith**, being much **more precious than** gold that perishes, though it is **tested by fire**, may be found to praise, honor, and glory at the revelation of Jesus Christ* (1Pet.1:6b-7).

I faced an unexpected test of my faith in 2005. I had just returned from a repentance conference with a group of close intercessors. This spiritual "test/attack" was actually the second one I had, as connected to this ministry trip. The first attack occurred while I was still attending the conference. I won't detail the first test, but will only share in summary. I had experienced a bizarre and incomprehensible sexual attack/temptation from an invisible power "occupying" my hotel bed, without my knowledge of its existence. This horrifying experience, which was like a bad movie, opened my eyes to understand how powerful the enemy is, and also to learn how to use the weapons of our warfare. Both the experiences of the first and second test are documented in my first book, "Coffee Talks With Messiah." In this current book about Fear, I will document only the second test.

We flew home from the conference late on a Saturday night. The flight home was long and delayed due to weather problems. After settling in with my family and unpacking, I got to bed rather late that night and was exhausted. The following experience happened at 1:00 AM, and I was sleeping peacefully.

Suddenly, I was jolted awake by a sensation of being freezing cold. At the same time, a thick and dreadful terror filled the room and was all around me, which caused me to shake. I was unable to move or speak, so great was the level of power upon me.

As I've partially shared with you in earlier chapters, I have known fear. I've been in serious car accidents and have suffered the phobia of cockroaches during my first seven years in Israel. I was once moments away from being assaulted on my college campus. The fear I have felt in the past was significant. But there is no vocabulary sufficient to describe the formidable, tangible terror I felt that night. It seemed alive. I pray I never feel anything like it again.

It is easier to discern this event in hindsight. The telling of this story gives us helpful information that I didn't have during the experience. Now, it may seem obvious that this fear could only have come from Satan. However, at that moment, awakened out of a deep sleep, I genuinely believed this was the "Spirit of the Fear of the Lord," named in Isaiah 11:1-3. In addition to Isaiah, there are also three passages in the

Book of Revelation which state that there are seven Spirits of God (see Rev.1:4, 4:5, 5:5).

I was familiar with Scriptures where our patriarchs felt a dreadful fear in God's Presence. When Abraham was about to receive the covenant of the Land of Israel, Genesis 15 records that "a thick and dread darkness" came over him. I knew that at Mount Sinai, a great terror came over the people when God descended to the mountain. Not only did the people tremble, but the mountain trembled as well. When Daniel saw a mighty angel, he fell on his face trembling and said that he could not even breathe.

My ancestors had felt the fear of the Lord at Mt. Sinai, and I believed He was teaching me what it meant to know the "Fear of the Lord." To me, this was a fully biblical aspect of God, and it didn't occur to me that Satan, or a powerful evil being, was in my bedroom, terrifying me with his tremendous power.

This fearful power did not remain at the same high level constantly, but it would decrease and then increase again. When it would fade slightly, I was able to speak; when it was at its most dreadful, I felt almost paralyzed. After lying in these waves of dread for almost half an hour, I began to think, by the prompting of His Spirit, *"What if this is not God?"*

During an interval while I was able to speak, I said, "If this fear is from God, give me the Spirit Test" (1Jn.4:2-3). I wanted to hear it clearly say that "Jesus Christ has come in the flesh," according to this biblical test of discernment. After a slight hesitation, an unpleasant voice answered me in a somewhat snarling tone, "Jesus Christ has come in the fle...sss..."

The last word trailed off without perfect clarity, but it managed to say the rest of the sentence. I thought the tone sounded too angry to be God, but I was very tired and wondered if God might be angry at me. Nevertheless, I was ready to rebuke it.

First, I said, "If this fear is not from the Lord God, I reject it and send it away, in Jesus' Name." Nothing changed, and I tried one other phrase, without success. It was hard for me to find the strength to speak, let alone use a strong and commanding tone with this presence. I mustered all my resolve and finally, I spoke with the authority that was needed. In a forceful tone, I used the phrase, **"The Lord rebuke you!"** (Jude 9) It instantly lifted off me, pulling back at high speed.

The atmosphere around me was replaced instantly with a visitation of God's true glory. First, I saw the clear blue heavens full of clouds; then a cross appeared in the clouds; then Yeshua was hanging on the cross with a light from heaven shining down on Him like a spotlight. Then I heard many voices say "Jesus Christ has come in the flesh" in a clear, sweet, almost musical tone. They said this phrase freely and happily, in stark contrast to the ugly snarl I had just heard a minute before. Then I lay in His true glory for a long time, which helped me to recover from the horrible fear which I had thought was God.

While I was in the Glory, the Lord showed me in a vision, the demon which had been in my bed at the hotel, a few days earlier. I was observing this hideous creature from a distance, and he could not see me. He was standing at the check-in counter at the hotel, as if he were a normal human guest, checking in. His head was large, bald, and ugly. His top half looked like a large, bare-chested human man, bulky, like a wrestler. His lower half was massive and reptilian, with a long tail. It was quite an education for me, to say the least.

I could not bear to imagine such an evil and repulsive being occupying my bed, let alone the disgust and remorse I would suffer if I had given it any satisfaction. If believers could see the unseen demonic powers who get gratification from making God's people fall into sin, they would not willfully indulge in secret sins, thinking they will ask for forgiveness later. What sacrifice will be left for their continual and deliberate sins? (Heb.10:26-27)

The Trumpet Sound of War!

When I wrote my second book, "A Prophetic Calendar: The Feasts of Israel," I reached the chapter on the first Fall Feast, called, "The Feast of Trumpets." This Feast is also called "Rosh HaShannah" by many, but I am emphasizing its more biblical name that means "The Blasting of the *Shofar*," or, "The Memorial of Blasting" (the ram's horn, or trumpet).

While I was still in the middle of writing this significant chapter, which represents the return of the Lord, I had a spiritual attack in a dream.

I had just returned from a long day of ministry, and I was sleeping that night. First, I dreamed I was writing this chapter on The Feasts of Trumpets (which I was also writing in real life). But as I wrote on my computer, the words kept disappearing, and paragraphs were being "stolen" by an invisible hand. I kept trying to put everything down in the computer, but the sentences kept changing, disappearing, and rearranging themselves. I was getting so frustrated and angry. Everything I did was being stolen and deleted before my eyes.

Then I heard an evil voice say, *"Little Bo-Peep has lost her sheep."* For those not familiar, there is a popular children's nursery rhyme about this little girl who can't find her sheep. I understood that the enemy was taunting me, taking away my precious words on the page. I knew I was that little girl, and he was stealing my sheep.

As soon as I heard this nursery rhyme quoted in an evil way, a great fear and terror came over me, as I was still sleeping. I partially woke up, and the great fear was still in the room. I began to do spiritual warfare.

As I was warring in my mind against this fearful evil, I was not able to drive it away. After a long, losing battle, I didn't know what more I could do, and I was tempted to give up. Then I felt the Holy Spirit show me to just **worship the Lord**, rather than continue to fight.

As I worshiped Him in my mind, ignoring the fear still upon me, I heard my daughter Keren's voice call out to me, "Goodnight, Mama!"

As I heard her sweet voice, I knew she was still awake, and if I called out to her, she would come into my room and pray for me, and this crushing evil would leave. I cried out her name as loud as I could: "**KEREN**!" Suddenly I was more awake, and the evil presence was gone.

Looking at the clock, it was almost midnight, and no one was at home besides Keren and me. I walked down the hall to her room, to tell her what had just happened to me, and how hearing her voice had saved me. However, she had actually been asleep for quite a while and **she had not said "Goodnight" to me, despite what my ears heard**.

It was the Lord, sending me her voice of comfort so that I could rally my strength, wake up, and escape from the onslaught.

Several days later, I thought I had finished writing the chapter, and I was waiting on the Lord. He told me to read Numbers 10, and He called my attention to verse 9.

When you go to war in your land against the enemy who oppresses you, then you shall **sound an alarm with the trumpets**, *and* **you will be remembered** *before the LORD your God, and* **you will be saved** *from your enemies* (Nu.10:9, NIV).

After reading this verse, the Lord reminded me of the attack I had experienced two nights earlier. As I recalled the midnight attack, the Lord showed me the warfare words of Moses, which he spoke, whenever the Ark would set out on the journey: *"Rise up, O LORD! May your enemies be scattered; may your foes flee before you"* (Nu.10:35, NIV).

He then asked me, *"What does Keren's name mean?"*

I was stunned as I realized the **other** meaning of her Hebrew name, *Keren Chen*. We had named her a "Ray of Grace." *Keren* means a <u>ray</u> of the sun, but its primary meaning in Hebrew is a HORN. Perhaps the sun's rays were named "horns," because of their shape, flaring out at the ends, like a horn. When King David used the phrase "the horn of my salvation," the Hebrew reads, *"keren yishi"* (Ps.18:2).

Through this experience and the Lord's explanation, He showed me that when I cried out Keren's name, it was like I was blasting the trumpet – I was **sounding the alarm**. In the passage above, God had promised to remember us and save us from our enemies when He heard the sound of the trumpet in a fierce battle. The moment I had cried out her name, "KEREN," I was awake and the evil presence vanished.

The Lord then gave me a weighty prophetic word about the end-time significance of the sounding of the trumpet, and His final "wake-up call" to His sleeping church. This word is shared in its entirety in my book, "A Prophetic Calendar: The Feasts of Israel."

Who Are We Contending With?

For though we walk in the flesh, ***we do not war according to the flesh****. For the* ***weapons*** *of our warfare* ***are not of our flesh****, but are* ***mighty in God*** *for pulling down strongholds,* ***casting down arguments*** *and every high thing that* ***exalts itself against the knowledge of God****, bringing every thought into captivity to the obedience of Christ* (2Cor.10:3-5, AP).

At times, there are certain people in our lives who torment us with intellectual-sounding challenges, mocking, arguments, and opposition to our beliefs, our lives, and our values. We think we are arguing with a person, and his or her human reasoning. We don't realize we are actually caught in an unwinnable argument with a spirit. We get caught up in frustrating disputes, whether with family members or colleagues, or even "difficult" believers we know, who should know better. But they are proud and stubborn, and they come against us.

For many long years, I suffered much from a close family relation, who would badger me for hours on end, concerning my faith. He would jump from evolution to social injustice, to sexual restrictions being unfair, to dinosaurs and Noah's ark, to the existence of Hell – no loving God could send people there – it seemed to be endless, the points he could repeat. He would alternate between seeming "open" to my points, but then always reverting back to mocking, cynical opposition. Though I kept trying to reason with him, because I loved him and was fighting for his salvation, I was at my wit's end, by the time each "conversation" ended. He would finally leave and go back to his home, but I felt like I was in a mental hospital. He would *seem* to grasp what I was saying about the Lord, but then, like a broken record, he would come right back with more of his incessant "babbling."

"Babble" is an interesting word. It means "to talk nonsense," or, to talk meaninglessly. To ramble in a confusing way, using logic that doesn't make sense. Many of the world's languages all share an almost identical word, which is closely related to the English word "babble." In all these languages, it means, "to speak nonsense." Amazing that we all agree on this one word of biblical origin! Think of it – many nations all agree on the one word that means "no nations can understand each other's language!"

We know that in early in Genesis, all the people groups and nations spoke a common language. But when they conceived the plan to build a tower to "heaven," for rebellious and idolatrous reasons, God came down to confuse their language. Thus, they would not understand each other's speech and would not be able to complete this demonic altar to "the gods."

In the Hebrew Bible, the word *"bab-el"* means "gate of God." It comes from an ancient Akkadian word. This is where the name of their city, "Babylon," comes from. The people wanted to build a gateway to their gods and to make contact with their false gods, who were demons. They set up this tower in opposition to the true Creator God. The Lord intervened and **confused their unified language**, so the people could no longer communicate. In modern Hebrew, the words for *"confuse"* or *"confusion"* are: *"balbel"* or *"bilbul."*

After many battles with my relative, I now believe there is an evil spirit of "babble," which speaks confusing and false words deliberately, to wear down and confuse a person who is arguing for righteousness and for God's requirements. This spirit leaves us in a fog of confusion, frustration, and feeling crazy. I now believe that my family member was allowing an evil spirit to use him to torment and mock me, always seeming to want more information from me, but never answering me, according to the truth I spoke.

At times, I felt like I was warring against a spirit, but I never started a confrontation. I just continued as if it were merely flesh and blood, during those years of misery. A few times, he threatened my life, just to prove that God wouldn't rescue me. But I felt he wouldn't really do it. Still, I didn't want to confront him. Maybe I was afraid the spirit would manifest violently, and I would be alone with a person much bigger and stronger than me, in my house.

The Lord is In Us, and We are In Him

*For **in Him** dwells all the **fullness of the Godhead** bodily; and **you are complete <u>in Him</u>**, who is the **head** of all **principality** and **power*** (Col.2:9-10).

Paul tells us that Yeshua is the **head** of wicked rulers in high places (principalities and powers). He has complete authority over evil beings.

And we too are fully equipped (complete) **in Him**, in Whom the **fullness of the Godhead dwells**. He has given us this same authority. How? **He lives in us,** and the enemy is **afraid** of us, if we **understand Who is living in us**!

*You are **of God**, little children, and have overcome them, because **He who is <u>in you</u> is greater than he who is <u>in the world</u>**...We know that **we are of God**, and the **whole world lies under the sway** of the wicked one* (1Jn.4:4, 5:19).

We are **of God** – we belong to Him. It is Satan who is in the world, and who exerts great influence over the world's people and its systems. The One who lives **in us** is far greater and stronger than the enemy, who is on **the outside**, and who can **never enter** our inner **holy sanctuary** with our Lord. When we are in severe distress, we must remember that the Lord **in us** is stronger than anything that can come against us from the outside. **His Spirit is the power on the inside**. We must remember this reality, or we might be beaten down, needlessly.

"He Has Nothing in Me"

*I will no longer talk much with you, for the ruler of this world is coming, and **he has nothing in Me*** (Jn.14:30).

Notice that the enemy has **nothing in Yeshua**. He has no foothold in His thoughts. No stronghold in His character, no weakness to exploit. Nothing that can lure Yeshua into disobedience or unholiness. Nothing the enemy can accuse Him of, before the Throne.

We too must let the Lord search our hearts, and ask Him if there is any foothold the enemy has **in us**. If so, it is our responsibility to consecrate our hearts and our motives. It's like our heart is a house with many rooms and closets. Do we have one unclean thing, hidden in a closet? If so, the enemy has a foothold in our home.

In the same way that we must rid our homes of idols and unclean things, we must also rid our hearts of anything from the enemy: our worldview, our opinions, our words. We must root out any area of our soul that gives the enemy a place in our heart that he can use against us. This is our voluntary choice, and the Lord won't root these things out by force. We all must be able to say, "The enemy has nothing in me."

Let me share one example from my own life, of how the Lord removed a black spot from my heart, and how I renounced a foothold that Satan had in my life, many years ago. The following is an excerpt from "Coffee Talks With Messiah," my first book.

Free to Conceive

"During our early months in Israel, I developed an urge to have a baby. At twenty-eight, I was responding to biological signals, and Israeli culture was very conducive to raising children....My husband suggested we wait until we were in our first 'real' apartment.

We attempted to conceive, and five weeks later, I was certain I was pregnant, but it turned out I was not, and I found myself very let down. Around this same time, I began a 21-day partial fast. My reasons for this lengthy fast were not connected to getting pregnant. I was preparing for my first trip back to the U.S. to visit my parents, and I knew I would encounter strong pressure from them to return home permanently. They had been very opposed to our move to Israel, so I was fasting to prepare my spirit to endure opposition and arguments for moving back.

While fasting, I was reading a book by Francis Schaeffer. I came to a section on 'original sin,' in which the author was discussing the curse upon Adam and Eve's bodies caused by their sin. The moment I read this, the Lord brought a strong Word of revelation to me about a curse I had placed on my own body, due to my sinful attitudes about children.

He began to remind me of many comments and attitudes I had learned from my parents about the inconvenience of children. They had often remarked that adults had more fun when the children were not around. I also remembered that while I was in graduate school, I had done a research paper on 'Child-Free by Choice' couples. This extensive research highlighted a number of couples who explained the multiple reasons why they had made the choice *never* to bear children. The advantages were numerous, including more money, more time, more vacations, and more time with one's spouse.

The Lord showed me a 'black' spirit over my heart in this area and gave me an immediate opportunity to repent on the spot. I fully repented at that moment, renouncing all wrongful belief systems and attitudes concerning children, and families with children. At that moment, I literally felt something dark leave my spirit. The Lord's Spirit instantly spoke to me, saying:

'You are now free to conceive.'

I do not exaggerate when I tell you that exactly forty weeks from that statement, I gave birth to our first child, an adorable blond son. We named him 'Raviv,' which means 'gentle rains,' from the book of Deuteronomy." [End excerpt].

The Enemy Comes When We are Vulnerable and Weak

The enemy doesn't play "fair." He will hit us when we're at our weakest, hoping to catch us on a bad day. We must always be vigilant, no matter what hardships we are going through.

About five years ago, I had a serious surgery, which went very well, but it was traumatic to my body. On the third day, they sent me home from the hospital, and I was told to rest quite a bit, until my body could heal. On that first early morning back at home, I was asleep.

At that time, I had two different frightening things that happened, both from the enemy. The first thing was this: I dreamed I saw the face of a boy, about 10 or 11 years old. He was close to me, right before my eyes. He looked very sweet, and he was smiling at me.

He looked at me and said, "I have a Word from the Lord for you."

I just looked at him, hoping to get a Word from the Lord.

He smiled triumphantly, and announced: "You have cancer!"

(Just to clarify, my surgery was not about cancer.)

I was instantly awake from this horrible declaration, and I knew if I didn't fight this evil word, I would enter a time of fear and would expect this terrible "word" to be real or true. I immediately rebuked this evil spirit, disguised as a nice boy, who I could no longer see, and I rebuked this evil "diagnosis."

I had to fight fear for a while after this, making sure I didn't give the enemy power over my life, my health, or my future. By doing warfare in my mind, the fear never developed, and the Lord has graciously and mercifully protected me since this event. This "word" was the enemy's will, but I had to believe it was not God's will. We must never agree with the enemy's will, or he will gain a foothold in us.

Special Note on Cancer and our Fear

So that there is no misunderstanding, I need to briefly highlight something. I am well aware that many precious believers in the Lord have fought battles with cancer, some of whom are (and were) close friends. Some are fighting now, as I write this. Some have won the battle, and some have lost it. I know that none of these dear friends "agreed" with having cancer. It just appeared in their body, and they were left to make the hard medical and spiritual decisions. I know they fought with every spiritual weapon possible, and many also followed every recommended medical procedure, as awful as these were.

Some chose not to accept any medical procedures and fought it out. One close friend succumbed to cancer, after an 8-year battle. She had refused all medical procedures. We cannot know if treatment could have changed the outcome, in her case. But her choice was to fight in the Spirit and with natural remedies. She did not seem to fear, and believed she would live. She continued to worship the Lord and do warfare in the Spirit. I respect her tremendously, though we lost her.

Some readers or their loved ones may be fighting this battle right now. I am not suggesting that cancer is ever the Lord's will for His beloved children. I do not believe it is His will, and I believe this disease is from the evil one. The enemy also has caused selfish, evil, or powerful people to put toxic chemicals in our air, our water and our food, which can result in more cancer cases than would ever normally occur. And then there are genetic issues that can increase risk in some populations, which I can only view as part of the fallen creation, and the fallen seed of sinful man, back to the Fall.

But I know that somehow, the Lord will sovereignly use the faith battle and spiritual wrestling to bring each one who suffers closer to His heart. In some cases, the pain and questions of "Why?" can drive people further from the Lord's heart, feeling He has abandoned them. It is easy to fall into this terrible state of mind, and I write with deep compassion in my heart, as any of us could think that He has abandoned us. But He has not.

I do not believe this vicious disease ever came from the Lord, nor that their own fears brought it upon them. This was not the point I was making, in sharing how I could not agree with the enemy's false diagnosis, given to me in an evil visitation.

Getting Free of a Mental Stronghold

If I had "received" and believed this awful word spoken to me by a demon who was disguised as a nice boy, it is possible I would have opened the door to worse things. It would have ruined my life if I had believed it. That false "word," sown by the enemy in the field of my heart, would have become a bad seed, corrupting my emotions with fear and bitterness. Do you see how important it is that the enemy "**has nothing in you**?"

The Lord said we are "Sons of Light." In Hebrew, there is an expression where someone is called a "Son of (something)." This means that we have those characteristics of whatever we are a "son of."

For example, Yeshua called James and John, "Sons of Thunder." We see an example of their brash and hot-tempered actions in Luke 9:49-55. They wanted to call down fire on the Samaritans, as Elijah had called down fire on the army captains who came to arrest him. They were "like thunder." John was young and had not yet matured into the perfect example of love that we see in his latter years. Oh, the power of Yeshua's redeeming love in all our hearts!

Judas Iscariot, who was later to betray Yeshua, was called, "the Son of Perdition." This is a terrible title because it means he is characterized by damnation or being lost forever.

So, for us to be "sons of light," it means we carry and display His light in this darkened world. He is the Light, and we are His "Sons of Light."

If you feel the enemy has something still in you, some foothold, or dark spot in your heart, ask the Lord. He will help you remove whatever bad seeds the enemy might have sown in your heart. Then your whole being will be full of light, and **the enemy will have nothing in you**.

You will likely have to renounce it, and speak the truth over your mind, will, and emotions. Then the Lord will mightily defend you since you are standing in agreement with His heart, so that this dark spot will have no further influence or hold over you. It can even be a seemingly insignificant thought embedded in your heart. For example:

"I am ugly."

"My life is meaningless."

"I am stupid."

"I am fat."

"No one cares about me. I was a 'mistake.' My parents didn't want me."

We must speak and agree with the Lord's thoughts about us, not the enemy's thoughts. Otherwise, the enemy has something in us, and it will destroy our destiny in God.

The Second Attack After Surgery

Another bad thing happened to me on the second early morning after coming home from the hospital. This shocking encounter will be the final testimony of this chapter, and of this book. Truth is stranger than fiction, as you will see in a minute.

I was sleeping, and in what seemed like a dream, I suddenly saw a young man sitting on the opposite side of my bed, bent over, facing away from me, facing the wall. He had brown skin, as if from another nationality. He was nearly naked, but because I was dreaming, I didn't have a second to analyze who this was, or what was he doing there. That thought was just not in my head. He immediately started talking to me, though he never turned his face towards me, seemingly talking down into his lap.

He told me he had found a good recipe, and said something about some grains and "oil" in the recipe. I personally do not like oily food, and so I answered him, saying that I was not a person who liked oil in my recipes. Apparently, I was opening a dangerous door by answering his "innocent" comment about a recipe, but of course, I couldn't figure that out at the moment.

The moment I answered him, the scene changed, and he was instantly on top of me, in one seamless movement, and this was no dream anymore. I was immediately waking up and thinking about what to do, as I wondered if this was an evil spirit. I was pretty sure this was not a real man, though it seemed real. I said the first thing I could think of, to stop him.

I said, "I'm married." Possibly, he would respect this.

He ignored this and continued his advance.

I was now very afraid, and the Holy Spirit must have put these words in my mouth:

"I'm married to Yeshua."

He stopped abruptly and looked at me strangely. His expression was puzzled and annoyed at being interrupted, like this was something he could never have imagined someone saying.

I said nothing more. He then was gone in an instant. He disappeared.

I thanked the Lord for the power of His jealous love over me. It didn't matter to this evil being that I was married in an earthly way. But being married to the Bridegroom of Heaven had an instant effect on him.

He was not permitted to touch the Lord's bride, once I made my case, and I marveled at this blessing and authority we carry. I loved the Lord more than ever, for He rescued me again!

I thought the evil spirit was gone, but about half an hour later, I looked and saw the back of him walking away from my room. I didn't realize he hadn't really left when he disappeared. He turned briefly, to look back at me with a look of disgust and anger, and then disappeared.

Remember that we are only married to Yeshua in our heart if we have a continual, open, and intimate relationship with Him. If I didn't have this consistent reality in my relationship with the Lord, my sentence, "I'm married to Yeshua," would not have defeated this demonic, seducing spirit. It's not a formula that delivers us. It is the reality of our bond with our Bridegroom King. Amen.

"For I am convinced that neither death nor life, neither angels nor demons, neither the present nor the future, nor any powers, neither height nor depth, nor anything else in all creation, will be able to separate us from the love of God that is in Christ Jesus (Messiah Yeshua) our Lord." (Rom.8:38-39).

Epilogue

*He will not be afraid of evil tidings
His heart is steadfast, trusting in the Lord.
Psalm 112:7*

I believe I have now reached the end of this journey, sharing all the Lord has put in my heart to encourage you, strengthen you, and to give you confidence that you will be counted as an Overcomer on that Day. That none of us will be counted as those who shrink back when the Lord looks at our soldierly hearts.

You may say, "How could I be a woman of valor? How could I be a man of valor? I have so many weaknesses and flaws – I do not consider myself to be a hero of high rank in the Lord's army."

I understand. I feel exactly the same as you do. However, the Lord does not measure us with human eyes. He does not scrutinize us with critical, fault-finding eyes. He gazes at us in wonder and joy, as He sees us trying to prepare our hearts for hard and treacherous times. He sees us trying to muster our resolve to refuse idolatry, lies, seduction, and the temptation to betray others to save ourselves when evil closes in. He knows we desire to be noble, brave, and selfless. But we do not feel that we measure up at this moment.

But Beloved of the Lord – He sees you with eyes of promise, eyes of hope, eyes of a future crown that has been laid up for you, with your name, and only your name on it.

He sees the sheaves of wheat you will gather in your arms and bring to your Heavenly Father, showing Him the fruit of your labors. And He will show you the high price you paid, the sacrifices you made, to be able to bring Him your fruit, your harvest, your sheaves of souls and brides and armies. Yes, He is looking at you, and all you will have gained before our race is finished.

This book is meant to strengthen and encourage you so that you and I can be just like King David. We can run after God's heart and find courage to do the impossible, just like David and his mighty men of valor. Just like Moses and Joshua, who could walk through dry and thirsty deserts for 40 years, and never despair of entering the Promise. Just like Caleb, at 80 years old, who could beg Joshua to let him go and kill a land full of literal giants, who were twice his size and weight. And Caleb did exactly what he promised Joshua, at 80 years old. Surely, the Lord can make brave warriors out of us, even me, the weakest of us all.

Remember the Kingdom Principle we learned in the first chapter. God chooses the unqualified and gives them an assignment that is "above them." He watches to see if we will obey, even though we feel unqualified. The very act of obeying Him, no matter how we feel about ourselves, will QUALIFY us to win the prize, the crown, the rewards offered in Revelation, Chapters 2 and 3.

"To you who will overcome, I will give all of the rewards promised in My Book." Read these chapters, Beloved, and see how great are the rewards for overcoming our fear.

We cannot do this alone, through our mental strength and resolve. We cannot overcome fear without the Lord's strength and courage living inside of us, and rising up like a bold lion at the moment we need Him the most. He will do it. He will never leave us or forsake us.

When we put our trust in Him alone, He will save us, even if we lose our temporal lives for a brief moment. It will be nothing, compared to Eternity in His heart of love. This life is a training ground, a school, a wilderness seminary – we will pass our test if we keep our eyes on the prize – Yeshua our Beloved King.

The Lord said to me, "No Fear for My People!" He means it, and I hope I have conveyed the tools and helps you will need to run your race with endurance, as I must also.

My love and blessings to all who read this book, and who allow the Scriptures to fortify us from the inside out.

Till we meet here, or in Eternity – my love to each of you,
Jill
June, 2019

Meditation on Scripture

Beloved of the Lord, as you read these Scriptures, put your name in them, personalize them and speak them over yourself. *"I will not fear the terror by night....a thousand may fall at my side, but it will not come near me..."*

Or, *"He'll give His angels charge over Jill, to keep Jill in all her ways."* Put your very own name in them.

Make these Scriptures your armor, and meditate on how real and powerful are these promises, and thousands more you can find in the Bible for yourselves. We will overcome by the Word of our testimony, by the Blood of the Lamb, and by not loving our lives, even to the point of death. We will make ourselves ready for that Day. Amen.

Psalm 91
He who dwells in the secret place of the Most High
Will abide under the shadow of the Almighty
I will say of the Lord, "He is my refuge and my fortress
My God in whom I trust."
Surely He'll deliver you from the fowler's snare
And from the deadly pestilence
He will cover you with His feathers
And under His wings you will find refuge
His truth will be your shield and buckler

You will not fear the terror by night
Nor the arrow that flies by day
Nor the pestilence that walks in darkness
Nor the plague that lays waste at noonday

A thousand may fall at your side
And ten thousand may fall at your right hand
But it shall not come near you, only with your eyes
You will see the reward of the wicked
Because you've made the Lord, who is my refuge
Even the Most High, your dwelling place
No evil shall befall you, nor shall any plague
Come near to you, to your dwelling place
He'll give His angels charge over you
To keep you in all your ways
In their hands they shall bear you up
You will not dash your foot against a stone

You will tread upon the lion and the cobra
The young lion and the serpent you will trample underfoot

Because he has set his love upon Me
Therefore I will deliver him
I will set him on high, because he has known My name
He will call upon Me, and I will answer him
I will be with him in trouble, I will deliver him
I will satisfy him with long life, I will honor him
And show him My salvation

Psalm 46:1-5,7
God is our refuge and strength
A very present help in trouble
Therefore we will not fear
Even though the earth be removed
And though the mountains be carried into the midst of the sea
Though its waters roar and are troubled
Though the mountains shake with its swelling
There is a river whose streams make glad the city of God
The holy place of the tabernacle of the Most High
God is in the midst of her, she will not be moved
God will help her, just at the break of dawn
The Lord of hosts is with us; the God of Jacob is our refuge

Psalm 62:5-8
My soul, wait silently for God alone
For from Him is my expectation
Only He is my rock and my salvation
He is my defense, and I will not be greatly moved
In God is my salvation and my glory;
The rock of my strength, my refuge is in God.

Psalm 27:1-3
The Lord is my light and my salvation
Whom shall I fear?
The Lord is the strength of my life
Of whom shall I be afraid?
When the wicked came against me, to devour my flesh
My enemies stumbled and fell
Though an army may encamp against me, my heart shall not fear
Though war may break out against me, even in this I will be confident.

1John 4:18
There is no fear in love; but perfect love casts out fear, because fear involves torment. But he who fears has not been made perfect in love.

2Tim.1:7
For God has not given us a spirit of fear, but of power and of love, and of a sound mind.

Psalm 23:4
Yea, though I walk through the valley of the shadow of death, I will fear no evil; for You are with me; Your rod and Your staff, they comfort me.

Psalm 3:3,5-6
But You, O Lord, are *a shield for me, my glory and the One who lifts up my head...I lay down and slept; I awoke, for the Lord sustained me. I will not fear ten thousands of people who have set themselves against me all around.*

Mt. 6:25
Therefore I say to you, do not worry about your life, what you will eat or what you will drink; nor about your body, what you will put on. Is not life more than food and the body more than clothing?

Psalm 33:18
Behold, the eye of the Lord is on those who fear Him, on those who hope in His mercy.

Psalm 34:7
The angel of the Lord encamps all around those who fear Him, and He delivers them.

1John 3:20-22
For if our heart condemns us, God is greater than our heart, and knows all things.
Beloved, if our heart does not condemn us, we have confidence toward God. And whatever we ask we receive from Him, because we keep His commandments and do those things that are pleasing in His sight.

2Cor.10:3-5
For though we walk in the flesh, we do not war according to the flesh. For the weapons of our warfare are not of our flesh, but are mighty in God for pulling down strongholds, casting down arguments and every

high thing that exalts itself against the knowledge of God, bringing every thought into captivity to the obedience of Christ.

*Several of these Scriptures for Meditation are the Author's Translation or Paraphrase

Appendix:
Will Yeshua Return and Reign on Earth for a Thousand Years?*

Some Christians do not believe there will be a **literal, thousand-year reign** of Yeshua on the earth, from His capital city, Jerusalem. Rather, they see all of history, since the resurrection of Yeshua, as a continual, spiritual "Millennium," which will continue till the "return of Christ."

This doctrine is called "*Amillennialism.*" In Latin, the prefix "*A*" means, "*without.*" Thus, the meaning of *Amillennial* is this: There will be no future thousand-year period on earth when Jesus will physically return to rule over the nations. This doctrine dates back to the 3rd, 4th, and 5th centuries. Some of the early church leaders who promoted this view were Origen, Jerome, Chrysostom, and Augustine.

The opposing doctrine is called "*Premillennialism.*" In Latin, the prefix "*pre*" means "*before.*" Thus, the meaning of *Premillennial* is this: We are still living in the age (time period) *before* the Lord returns to earth for a thousand years. We believe in the Lord's literal return in His glorified body; He will rule over the leaders and nations of this world, from the city of the Great King: Jerusalem.

During the 1st and 2nd century, most writings of the original disciples of Yeshua, as well as the generation who followed after them, reflected a Premillennial view. These included the apostle John, Bishop Papias of Hierapolis, and Justin Martyr.

We'll examine many Scriptures that testify of the establishment of the Lord's future throne in Jerusalem. He will rule the nations as the "greater David," with zeal and justice, and with "a rod of iron," as we see in Psalm 2, and also in Revelation 2.

Revelation 20 provides the strongest biblical evidence for a literal thousand-year reign of Messiah. When we study other prophetic Scriptures, we find more evidence that the Lord will return as our righteous King-Messiah. Let's take a moment to document the trustworthiness of the Premillennial view.

*They lived (came alive) and **reigned with Christ for a thousand years**...they shall be priests of God and of Christ, and shall reign with Him a thousand years* (Rev.20:4-6).

In the passage below, we see an astonishing promise from the Lord to His overcoming believers. He is quoting Psalm 2 – the very promise His

Father gave to Him: to rule over the nations with a rod of iron. **But now,** He promises that **same authority** and **rod of iron to us**! This is an awesome proof of a literal Millennial reign on the earth. In Heaven, the nations don't need to be dashed to pieces like pottery! Only on earth do they need firm discipline.

*And he who overcomes, and keeps My works until the end, to him **I will give power (authority) over the nations – 'he shall rule them with a rod of iron; they shall be dashed to pieces like the potter's vessels'** – just as I also have received from My Father* (Rev.2:26-27).

Revelation 20 uses the phrase "one-thousand years" six times. During this time, King Yeshua will enforce righteousness on earth. We will partner with Him as kings and priests, and He shares His government with us (see Mt.19:28; Lk.22:29-30; 2Tim.2:12; Rev.3:21; 5:10).

This comes right after Revelation 19, where we see the Son of Man coming as the Captain of the Hosts of Heaven, riding forth in majesty. His robes are stained with blood (see Isa.63:1-4), as He inflicts vengeance on the rebellious. This millennial era begins when the Lord returns to earth, in a hostile takeover of the raging and rebellious nations (see Psalm 2). This is a literal event that we will see with our own eyes. It is not mystical or figurative. Neither was His first coming. Both are historical, literal events we have both seen, and will see, in real time, geography and history.

There is no biblical reason to spiritualize either Revelation 19 or 20. Let's be logical:

1. If the Lord Jesus is already ruling and reigning as King over the earth, from Heaven, since the time of His resurrection (as the Amillennial position claims)…

2. And if no further earthly Kingship was necessary…

3. Why would He reveal His **future** Millennial reign to the Apostle John, **50 years after His resurrection?**

4. Revelation 20:3 tells us that Satan will be bound and shut away **so that he can no longer deceive the nations until the thousand years are over.** Can anyone say that Satan is no longer free to deceive the nations?

He is deceiving the nations continually, which is obvious to anyone who is paying attention. Therefore, this thousand-year period, when Satan will be imprisoned and unable to deceive the nations, has not yet happened, since the resurrection of the Lord until now.

If we are already living in the "figurative" Millennial Reign of Messiah, and if Satan is already figuratively bound, why are children being sexually abused and sold as slaves? Why are evil governments being deceived into passing wicked laws, framed in iniquity? Why are millions of Christians addicted to pornography? Why is injustice rampant, and why is the global persecution of the saints at the highest levels in history? Why are millions going to hell?

Doesn't the Scripture tell us that when Yeshua returns, He will rule the earth with a rod of iron? Revelation tells us that when **His Kingdom comes to the nations of the earth**, punishment will be poured out on the wicked (see Rev.11:15-18). Justice is the scepter of His Throne.

But on earth, there is no justice and "truth has fallen in the streets" (see Isa.59:14-15). Wickedness is increasing, and justice is nowhere to be found. Where are His zeal and His strength? Where is His rod of iron? Why is blasphemy, child-sacrifice, witchcraft, and demonic worship tolerated?

No, the Righteous One is **not** reigning over the earth. **Man** is reigning over the earth, and doing whatever is "right in his own eyes." Man was given six days (6,000 years) to rule the earth. But the 7th Day belongs to the Lord. The seven-thousandth year belongs to the Son of Man, and He **will** reign as the Last Adam – the Man without sin.

Daniel saw the Son of Man brought before the Ancient of Days and crowned with dominion over all the people, nations and languages of the earth.

*One like **the Son of Man**…came to the Ancient of Days… to Him was given…a kingdom, that all peoples, nations, and languages should serve Him…The kingdom… shall be given to the people, the saints of the Most High* (Dan.7:13-14, 27).

The Earth and Nature will be Healed

During the Millennium, the earthly elements of nature (land, water, sky and animal life) will still function in Israel and in the earth, but there will be a supernatural cleansing, healing and restoring of all these elements. Here are a few biblical examples of how this will look:

Ezekiel saw the cleansing of the Dead Sea, and the healing waters were flowing in the river from Jerusalem to the salt Sea. He saw the trees and fruit on the Millennial earth; and the leaves were for the healing of the nations. This is not a heavenly scenario. There is no Dead Sea in heaven. This is Heaven on earth – the Millennium!

There was water flowing from under...the temple...He said to me: "This water flows...when it reaches the sea (Dead Sea), its waters are healed...Along the bank of the river...will grow all kinds of trees used for food...they will bear fruit every month, because their water flows from the sanctuary. Their fruit will be food, and their leaves for medicine." (Ezek. 47:1-12).

Isaiah saw the human lifespan extended much longer, almost like the incredible longevity before the flood.

"For the child shall die one hundred years old, but the sinner being one hundred years old shall be accursed. They shall build houses...and they shall plant vineyards...As the days of a tree, so shall be the days of My people...The wolf and the lamb shall feed together..." (Isa.65:20-25)

Enmity and violence between animals, and also between animals and humans, will be removed and the peace restored (see Rom.8:20-21).

The wolf also shall dwell with the lamb...the calf and the young lion and the fatling together; and a little child shall lead them. The cow and the bear shall graze..." (Isa.11:6-7).

The Lord Yeshua's government will progressively spread to all nations (see Isa.9:7).

Yes, all kings shall fall down before Him; all nations shall serve Him (Ps.72:11).

Jerusalem will be Cleansed and Restored

When the Lord has washed away the filth of the daughters of Zion, and purged the blood of Jerusalem from her midst, by the spirit of judgment and by the spirit of burning, then the Lord will create above every dwelling place of Mount Zion, and above her assemblies, **a cloud and smoke by day and the shining of a flaming fire by night.**

For over all the glory there will be a **covering***. And there will be a* **tabernacle** *for shade in the daytime from the heat, for a place of refuge, and for a shelter from storm and rain* (Isa.4:4-6).

After the final, most destructive war, when Jerusalem lies in ruins, stained with the blood of the slain, the Lord Himself will purge and purify the remnant of Israel. He will cover every home and meeting place with His **cloud of smoke and cloud of fire** – as in the days of the wandering in the wilderness. Over all this glory, there will be a "covering." The Hebrew word for "covering" in this text is *"Chuppah,"* which means "a Wedding Canopy." He will be a Husband to Israel, once again. And He will set up a permanent Tabernacle for shade from heat and rain. In Heaven, there is no need for physical protection from heat and rainstorms. This is on earth, Beloved. This is the beginning of the restorative work of the Millennium, beginning in Jerusalem, and spreading to all the nations.

Who is On the Lord's Side?

The millennial kingdom is one of the major revelations of Scripture. It fulfills God's destiny for the earth and His people living on the earth. The New Testament makes it clear that the kingdom is already here (in a limited way), but is not yet fully here until the Lord returns to make all things right. Come, Lord Yeshua!

Although we are surely called to exercise our authority and to take up the weapons of our warfare against the devil, *it does not erase the literal truth of the Word of God*: The Lord Himself will return and will reign for a thousand years. **Only the Lord can rule perfectly, judge, restore, and rebuild this defiled and corrupted earth, staggering under the heavy weight of our sin.**

The LORD said to my Lord, **"Sit at My right hand, till I make Your enemies Your footstool."**

The LORD shall send the rod of Your strength out of Zion*. Rule in the midst of Your enemies!*

Your people shall be volunteers in the day of Your power; *In the beauties of holiness, from the womb of the morning, You have the dew of Your youth.*

The LORD has sworn and will not relent, "You are a priest forever, according to the order of Melchizedek."

The Lord is at Your right hand; **He shall execute kings in the day of His wrath.**

He shall judge among the nations, He shall fill the places with dead bodies, He shall execute the heads of many countries.

He shall drink of the brook by the wayside; therefore He shall lift up the head. (Ps.110).

AMEN.

*The biblical teachings in this Appendix were enhanced greatly by the comprehensive scholarship of Pastor Mike Bickle. I am indebted to him for so many teachings; and in this case, for his teachings and writings on historical Premillennialism. www.ihopkc.org

About the Author

Jill Shannon is a Messianic Jewish Bible teacher, author and worshiper/songwriter. She has authored seven books, twelve worship CDs and a 12-part DVD teaching series. Her fourth book and DVD teaching series are called, *"Israel's Prophetic Destiny: If I Forget Jerusalem."* Jill's most recent book is "The Priestly Songwriter," a spiritual and technical guide to composing worship songs. Check Jill's website for all books, music, and teachings. www.jillshannon.org

Jill currently speaks and writes about the worship of Heaven, holy living, intimacy and transparency with the Lord, the biblical Feasts, the Song of Songs, Israel, and the Church. Her latest CD's are: *"Home to My Father"* (2017), and *"Jerusalem"* (2018). Her newest worship CD is *"Eternal Now,"* released in June, 2019.

Jill is married, with three grown children and two grandsons. To order or learn more about her books and listen to clips from her worship CD's, and to listen to free teachings, go to her website. To contact Jill, email: jill@coffeetalkswithmessiah.com

About Manifest Publications

Manifest Publications is the publishing division of Manifest International, LLC. Our objective is to help like-minded ministries and writers produce and distribute materials which proclaim the Gospel of Jesus Christ to all the world and equip the global Church for unity and maturity.

www.manifestinternational.com
www.manifestbookstore.com